Designing Fate

John Sandes

Designing Fate

Copyright © 2012 by Indo-European Publishing

Contact:
IndoEuropeanPublishing@gmail.com

The present edition is a reproduction of 1901 publication of this work, produced in the current edition with completely new, easy to read format by Indo-European Publishing.

For an authentic reading experience, the Spelling, punctuation, and capitalization have been retained from the original text.

Cover Design by Indo-European Design Team

ISBN: 978-1-60444-610-4

IndoEuropean
Publishing.com
Los Angeles, CA, USA

CONTENTS

AUTHOR'S NOTE

In searching for the wreck of the Australian steamer Elingamite, which was lost on the "Three Kings"—afterwards found to have been incorrectly charted—a diver employed by Lloyd's agent, who was endeavouring to recover the specie sunk in the vessel, came upon the wreck of an unknown steamer that had evidently struck the same rocks many years earlier and had disappeared. The diver reported to the puzzled salvage expert that he had located the Elingamite, and in confirmation of his claim he produced rusty tools brought up out of the sunken steamer. After further diving operations a second steamer was found on the ocean floor, and proved to be the Elingamite. But the identity of the steamer which had been wrecked long years previously on the same rocks was never established. That strangely dramatic discovery, which was recounted by Lloyd's agent to the author suggested the main idea of this story.

CHAPTER I

A RUDE AWAKENING

"A bad business, my boy; a very bad business. I cannot tell you how sorry I am for you."

The old colonel stroked his white moustache and stared abstractedly at the matting. The clock on the mantelpiece of the colonel's working room in the bungalow ticked on, and the young man with the blue eyes, brown curly hair, and soldierly figure said never a word. His face was very grey, and there was a whole world of suffering in his eyes.

"When you were attached to the regiment for training, just a year ago, McLean," continued the old colonel, "I looked up your Australian record, and I was proud of you. Your dead father was one of my oldest friends, and I rejoiced for his sake in your successful career. Colonel Blakeway, your commanding officer, was at Sandhurst with me many years ago, and when he wrote to me suggesting your name as that of an Australian subaltern to be attached to the regiment for training, I immediately assented. I felt sure that it would have pleased your dead father if he could have known that his son was serving the Queen under myself."

Something like a dry sob escaped from the soldierly young officer, but he quickly mastered himself.

"I am deeply grateful to you, sir," he said; "and I can assure you that the stain which has fallen upon my father's name is what grieves me most in the whole of this miserable business."

Colonel Elmslie, of the Forty-first Pathans, in cantonments at Tilgit, rose from his chair and paced slowly up and down the room in manifest agitation.

"My boy," he said, "a wise man never criticises the conduct of another man's wife, and if you were a stranger to me I should doubtless take the safe and easy course of declining to intervene in this matter at all, but my long friendship with your dead father and my pride and interest in your own career make it impossible for me

1

to look on with unconcern when that career is being ruined by a woman who is—forgive me if I wound you—unworthy to be your wife."

The young officer straightened himself into rigidity, as though to bear a physical blow.

"And I have only been married for two months," he whispered with dry lips.

"My boy," said the old colonel in a tone of deep sympathy, as he stopped his pacing up and down the room and placed his right hand on the young officer's shoulder, "there is nothing to be gained, believe me, by shirking trouble. Better far to face the situation like a soldier. The woman who fascinated you when you first met her on the mailboat between Colombo and Bombay, whom you married two months ago in a frenzy of boyish passion, and who was detected last night in a flagrant piece of cheating at cards in Major Mortimer's bungalow, is not unknown in India. My wife met her some years ago at Simla. Mrs. Harrington, as she then was, possessed a sinister reputation, and when poor Tom Harrington died she disappeared, and was not seen again until you brought her up here two months ago as your wife, having married her while you were on temporary leave. No one here except my wife had ever met her, or could identify her with Mrs. Harrington. We resolved to accept her for your sake, hoping that her early reputation was undeserved, and that she would make you happy. Nobody could be more grieved than I am that you married in haste without letting even me, your father's old friend, know of your intention. For I might have saved you from an irreparable mistake and the regiment from a most unpleasant scandal."

The young officer turned deadly white. "What course do you wish me to adopt, sir," he said, "in the interests of the regiment?"

"I do not wish to put it on that ground, McLean," said Colonel Elmslie, not unkindly. "But I think that in your own interests it would be better for you to leave Tilgit as soon as possible, and to take your wife away from India. Fortunately, the period of twelve months for which you were attached to us has almost expired. In the report which it will be my duty to furnish to the military authorities in Australia upon your work here I shall make no reference whatever to your domestic affairs, which do not concern me officially. And you may rest assured that I shall express the very highest possible opinion of your soldierly qualities, unremitting diligence in all the duties of your profession, and splendid gifts of leadership. I wish, my boy, that our parting could be a happier one, but you are young, and you will outlive, I trust, all the painful consequences of a mistake into which you were led by youthful passion and ignorance of the world."

"Thank you, Colonel, for your kindly advice," said the young officer in a broken voice. He wrung the proffered hand in silence, and, half-dazed by the shame and misery of it all, groped his way to the door.

When the colonel was having tiffin with his wife a few minutes later, Mrs. Elmslie, who had already heard the whole sordid story of the scandal from her most intimate friend, Mrs. Mortimer, could not help referring to it. Her worldly old heart had in it a streak of motherliness which was touched by the terrible distress of the young Australian officer.

"Fred," she said to the colonel, "can nothing be done to save that young fellow from this appalling disgrace? His only crime has been that he loved that wretched woman with callow infatuation, and married her without knowing anything whatever about her. Surely something might be done to save him from having his whole life ruined by the idiocy that made him blunder into marriage with a woman ten years older than himself who is nothing more than a common swindler."

"I put it to him as gently as I could, my dear," said the practical old colonel with his mouth full of curry. "But the whole thing was so flagrant. Mortimer actually saw her drop her handkerchief and pick up the ace of diamonds with it—like any common card-sharper. She was caught with the ace in her hand, and the discard—a small club—on the floor at her feet. How can a thing like that be hushed up? The only thing for them both to do is to disappear as soon as possible."

"But surely the story won't be allowed to leak out, Fred. It would be too awful for the poor fellow if it did."

"I can only say that I have done everything possible to stop it, my dear. There were only seven people in the room altogether when the thing happened. Mortimer and Stanhope were standing out, and the five who were playing were Mrs. Mortimer, Mrs. Burlington, Carvill, Sykes-Huntington, and Mrs. McLean. There were four men and two women besides the culprit. I have seen them all, and each individual gave me a sacred promise that the matter would be kept an inviolable secret."

"That was a capital idea of yours, Fred," said Mrs. Elmslie.

"But I find that one of them has already told you," retorted the colonel grimly.

"Well, surely that is no harm," said Mrs. Elmslie pleasantly. "I hope I can be trusted to keep a secret. It's a pity that Mrs. Burlington was there, though, because she is sure to tell Mrs. Abbott, and Harry Abbott is certain to mention it to his particular pal Harford-Clinton at the club, and it will be all round Tilgit before the gymkhana on Thursday."

Colonel Elmslie groaned. "Well, at any rate I have done my best to save poor young McLean from the wolves," he said; and then, as he poured another peg into the tall glass, he added: "There's a mistake in the system somewhere. It's all very well to train up a boy in all the military virtues from childhood, and expect him to grow into a combination of Napoleon and St. Anthony; but when the woman comes along, what happens to the regulations? As long as there are petticoats in the world, my dear, there will be trouble."

"Don't be coarse, Fred," said Mrs. Elmslie with an indulgent smile.

"That's not coarseness," returned the colonel; "it's common sense. Look at the case of this unfortunate young McLean. They put him through the mill—junior cadets, senior cadets, drill,

4

manoeuvres, and all the rest of it, so rigorously that he had no time to think of anything but his drill-book. Consequently, the first woman who snapped her eyes at him bagged him. And it was bad luck for him that she happened to be a woman who had fallen so low as to be mixed up with card-sharpers working the mailboats between Aden and Bombay."

"It's rather sad though, all the same, isn't it, Fred?" said Mrs. Elmslie, whose little golden vein of genuine feeling was hidden in the conglomerate of worldliness, conventionality, and self-interest that made up the greater part of her nature. "However, the young man will no doubt go back to his home in Australia at once, and I hear that the divorce laws over there are extremely liberal. It's to be hoped that it will not take him long to get rid of his incubus."

"Hum!" said the colonel. "Not a cheerful description of a bride of two months, is it, my dear? Hullo! why, bless my soul, I have to be at the polo-ground at two."

And away he clanked.

But for Hector McLean the daily routine of pleasure and duty at Tilgit was at an end.

As he rode slowly away to his own bungalow on the outskirts of the station, he revolved in his mind the maddening realities of his position. And no matter from what point he started, he reached always the same wretched termination. His brief married life, it was clear, had ended in a cul de sac. The most painful scene of all had yet to be lived through. It was necessary for him to tell his wife, who had deceived him and disgraced him, that they must leave India.

And what of his career—the career for which he had worked so steadfastly since he first joined the junior cadets in his schooldays in distant Australia? Was his life as a soldier to be wrecked as well as his life as a private citizen? Were the confident predictions of the instructional officers who had prophesied a brilliant future for him to be falsified? Was he to pass into the ignominious list of those who had failed to come up to the standard of character demanded by the military authorities from all those who sought to serve their country as officers? To a man of merely

5

average character and application the blow would have been a severe one. To such a man as Hector McLean, whose whole faculties had been concentrated upon the attainment of success in his military career until he met Mildred Harrington, the shock was well-nigh paralysing.

He rode slowly along the dusty track, entirely oblivious of outer surroundings, and when his charger stopped in front of the gate of his compound, McLean dismounted mechanically, handed the bridle to the waiting sais, and strode up to the verandah, where a tall dark-haired woman, seated in a low chair, was feverishly turning over the leaves of a three-months-old illustrated paper. The deathly pallor of her skin and the dark rings round her eyes told of a troubled night.

"Well," said the woman, looking up defiantly; "what did the old fool want to see you about?"

"There should be no need for you to ask why the colonel sent for me," replied her husband quietly. "He knows everything that occurred last night. He has promised to keep the—the—disgraceful incident a secret in order to save the regiment from scandal."

"What rubbish you are talking!" broke in the woman angrily. "It was a mere accident. Dozens of people do the same thing every night of the week, and because it is not noticed nobody cares a rap." She was talking very fast, and Hector McLean eyed her gravely.

"Surely, Mildred, you are not thinking of what you are saying," said McLean sternly. His wife seemed to be bereft temporarily of a moral sense. "Are you incapable of seeing that cheating at cards is a particularly despicable form of theft?"

Then the woman flared up. Half hysterical after the long torturing sleepless night, she rose from the chair and faced her husband furiously. "Oh, you make me sick, sick, sick, with your miserable goody-goody twaddle!" she cried. "Two months ago you told me that you loved me and could not live without me. To-day you tell me that I am a thief. You came into my life and dragged me away from the friends who admired me and made much of me, to bring me up to this hole, where all the old cats avoid me as if I had the plague. And because I happened to make a little mistake over a

6

miserable game of cards you turn from me like the rest of them. What do they want to do with me now—to send me to prison or only to Coventry? I insist upon knowing. I demand to be told at once. Life isn't so amusing up in this God-forsaken place that it won't be a blessed relief to get back to civilisation, and the sooner the better, as far as I am concerned."

Hector McLean stood appalled at the unreasoning and hysterical outburst. "As soon as you can control yourself," he said firmly, "I will tell you what has to be done."

"For goodness' sake, go on," said the woman, stamping her foot. "Even a prisoner has a right to know the sentence of the court without being kept in suspense longer than necessary. And after all you are my husband, don't forget that. The law will compel you to support me, even if you have forgotten your vows of eternal love after two months—only two months!"

She gave a slight shudder and turned her gaze outwards across the dusty road, and the banyans and the club compound to the towering mountain peaks that almost enclosed the lonely station, producing the effect of a gigantic prison for the little handful of white men and white women encamped there.

"Sit down in that chair, Mildred, and listen to me," said McLean in his resolute, low-pitched voice, "for there is something which must be said by me to you, here and now."

The woman sat down on the edge of the chair, leaning forward, with her face resting on her hands and her elbows on her knees. In her eyes was a look of tense and painful expectancy. She felt the strength of the man's will at last. It held her in silence, as though she were spent and exhausted after the rush of babbling words a moment earlier.

"Listen to me, Mildred," said the young man in his steady even voice. "It is necessary for us both to leave Tilgit at once. We must go away from here; we must get out of India."

"Rubbish!" said the woman angrily. "You can't go. You have your career to think about."

"My career is over so far as India is concerned," said McLean, with a trace of bitterness in his tone. "Possibly it is over altogether.

7

Well, it can't be helped now. But you are my wife, and I intend to stand by you. If we cannot live here we can live in another country."

"I don't want to go to any other country," said the woman wearily. "I am sick to death of travelling. I want to stay in one place and have what I have never had yet—a home."

"I can give you a home, Mildred, in my own country—in Australia, where I was born, where all my friends are, and where I had hoped to do some useful work before I die. Soldiering is a man's game, after all. I suppose that is why I chose it. You will come back with me to Australia, and together we will live down this terrible thing. There now, you mustn't cry, Milly. It will all come right in the end."

"Oh don't, Hector! Don't speak kindly to me! It's more than I can bear." The woman's body was shaken with sobs; she threw herself into the chair and buried her face in her hands.

Hector McLean was down on his knees beside her at once, comforting her. "A man must stick to his wife, Milly, even if she does make a mistake," he said. "We will forget all this when you come with me to Caringal. You know that my mother died when I was a child, and my father soon followed her. I shall be all alone with you at Caringal, and I shall always be able to get a military job of some sort, I suppose."

The unhappy woman was weeping unrestrainedly now. "Oh, I know I'm a bad lot, Hector, a rotten bad lot; but when you came into my life I meant to turn over a new leaf. Indeed I did. But now it is all over. I cannot imagine what made me cheat last night. The idea came into my head quite suddenly that it would be so easy to bring off that stale old trick. Almost before I realised what I was doing, it was done. And then came the exposure."

Mildred McLean had never looked less attractive. Her eyes were red, her cheeks were haggard, and her lips were quivering. Though really only thirty-two, she looked fully forty. But her boyish husband experienced a sharp revulsion of feeling as his eyes dwelt on her face. Here was a woman surely who was a strange contradiction—a woman capable of thoughtless, careless evil-doing, but also of true greatness, of heroic self-sacrifice. The sense of shame and outraged justice ebbed from his heart and a wave of love and pity rushed in. True, she had done a base act. But was she wholly base? His heart said no.

"Come inside now, dear, for I have many things to do," he said, stroking her hand, but when he tried to raise her up he saw that she had fainted.

Muhammad Bahksh, the "khansama," was wise in the ways of mem-sahibs. He brought burnt feathers and brandy in a wine-glass. And then he helped Hector McLean to carry his bride of two months into the bungalow, where Shaibalini, Mrs. McLean's ayah, was waiting. McLean laid his wife on her bed, and she opened her eyes and smiled wanly at him. "I often feel like that now, dear," she said, "but I shall be all right in a minute."

But Muhammad Bahksh, as he listened to a few hastily muttered sentences that Shaibalini the ayah poured into his ear, looked preternaturally wise.

"The eyes of the sahib are blind," he replied, "because of his want of knowledge. But we know what we know."

Next morning Colonel Elmslie received information that the Zakka Khels were hiding their wives and families in caves in the hills—the usual preliminary to an extended raid. The tribesmen had been exhibiting more than usual unrest, and at least a dozen rifles belonging to the Forty-first Pathans had disappeared.

"It's just the job for McLean before he goes," muttered the colonel thoughtfully; "and besides, it will take his thoughts off his own troubles."

So McLean cantered away at the head of fifty native troopers, each of whom had the light of battle in his eyes and rations for three days in his saddle-bags.

It was in the days before the gun-runners of the Persian Gulf had distributed arms to all the potential enemies of Great Britain in the tribesmen's country. Stolen rifles at that time fetched high prices among the hillmen.

When the young Australian returned to Tilgit with his troop on the fourth day, with ten of the missing rifles and a bullet-hole through his helmet, he found his wife gone.

Muhammad Bahksh explained that the mem-sahib had gone out for a ride immediately after his departure. She had not yet returned. However, she had left a chit on the dressing-table.

This was the chit:—

"MY DEAREST HUSBAND,—Do not be angry with me for going away. You made me happier than I ever thought I could be in my whole life, but it is all over now. By one mad act I threw away all the happiness that you gave me, and now I must leave you. If I were to remain with you your career would be ruined. I have seen too much of the world to believe that the possession of an impossible wife is no bar to advancement. You would be dragged down by your unfortunate marriage. But if I am not with you the way will be open to you. I shall watch your career from far away. I shall follow each promotion through the newspapers, and be proud of your success. But you must never see me again. I thank you, dear, from my heart for all that you have given me—your love, your name, and your protection. It is for your sake that I give up everything. I cannot accept the sacrifice that you have offered me. After all, a man's work is a man's life. If nobody in Australia knows that you married me your career will be a brilliant one. If you are hampered with me you will never rise at all. And so I cannot hesitate. Do not worry about me. Do not follow me. Try to forget me. I have the fifty pounds you gave me on my birthday, and out of India I can get work as a governess or a companion. Remember that I shall always watch your career with loving pride, and that I shall always think of you with tears of gratitude for the honest boyish love that you, gave me. And now goodbye. I'm sure you have not forgotten the song I sang on the first night that I met you—'I love you so, dear, that I only can leave you' I little thought that it would so soon come true.

"Your unhappy
"MILDRED."

Hector McLean read the letter through and passed his hand in bewilderment across his forehead.

Then he summoned Muhammad Bahksh.

10

"The mem-sahib has gone down to Bombay to wait for me," he said slowly to the khansama. "Lay my kit out ready for packing. We are going back to Australia together."

CHAPTER II

THE ADOPTION

"Well, this is a delightful surprise, Grace, dear [hugs], for I thought you were hundreds of miles away, looking out on a vast expanse of sheep [more hugs] and utterly forgetful of civilisation. Come up to my room at once, and powder your nose and tell me all about it—how long you are going to stay, and what you intend to do to amuse yourself."

Laura Martin, the capable and by no means bad-looking proprietress of the fashionable St. Kilda boarding-house known as 'The Cedars,' waited until the cabman had deposited Mrs. Hesseltine's portmanteau in the hall and taken his departure. Then she placed her hand lightly on Grace Hesseltine's waist and convoyed her upstairs to a large, lofty room, with a balcony overlooking the bay.

Sitting on the edge of the bed while Mrs Hesseltine removed her hat and her travelling cloak and powdered her nose at the dressing-table, Laura Martin, who had been one of the big girls at the Presbyterian Ladies' College when Grace first attended that august seat of feminine culture, poured out innumerable questions.

"How is Simon?"

Mrs. Hesseltine admitted that Simon was getting old and shaky. His temper did not improve with age, but there was no real vice about him and he never went off his feed. "He just roams about the paddocks," she added, "and when I go out on the verandah with a drink for him, he comes up to me at once."

It appeared presently that Simon was not a horse but a husband. Grace had married him soon after she left school, when she was eighteen and he was fifty-seven; now she was twenty-three and he was sixty-two. Latterly, she had begun to doubt, with a persistence that increased daily, whether it was worth while to be the mistress of Mindaroona if one had to have Simon as well.

"You used to get on with him all right," said Laura Martin, with a vague feeling that her friend was not being quite frank with her. "He's not any worse than he has always been, is he?" she asked sympathetically.

"Not a bit, dear," said Mrs. Hesseltine disconsolately, eyeing the reflection of her pretty face in the mirror with as much interest as if she had never seen it before.

"Well, then, you must buck up, old girl," retorted Laura Martin genially. Most of her paying guests were men, and her conversation was apt to show distinct traces of the fact. "Buck up, and have a good time while you can. You'll be a long time dead, remember."

"It's all very well for you, Laura," replied Mrs. Hesseltine with a distinct quiver at the corner of her mouth. "You have regular occupation here, with your business to run, and constant bustle and variety. When your husband died and you started this boarding-house you were as mournful, morbid, and moping a widow as I ever saw, and just look at yourself now—buxom, jolly, always laughing, and much better looking than you ever were before. It's having regular work to occupy your mind with, I suppose, and lots of men always around you, too."

"You shocking young woman! You'll be calling me a female Mormon next."

"Well, just think how different it is with me. Nobody to talk to but Simon and the maids. Nothing to see but sheep. Nothing to think about but—oh, I can't stand it any longer—I can't, I can't!"

Mrs. Grace Hesseltine, of Mindaroona, N.S.W., mopped her pretty eyes openly with her handkerchief, and in an instant Laura Martin was beside her, and had slipped a sustaining arm round her waist. "You mustn't talk like that, dear," she said. "Tell me all about it. Two heads are better than one, you know."

"But you wouldn't understand, dear," said Grace. "You're so different from me, and you would only think me a fool."

"No, indeed," said Laura. "I think I can guess what it is, Grace," she went on as she smoothed the soft hair of the younger woman almost maternally. "Tell me, dear, tell me!"

"I want a child," said Mrs. Hesseltine, with a despairing note in her voice. "I want a little baby to kiss and love and talk to. I cannot go on living at Mindaroona any longer without one. I am terrified that I shall kill myself some day, Laura, out of sheer misery and loneliness."

"Hush, dear, hush!" said Laura. "Now, I'm just going to make you stay here with me for at least a month, and we'll soon brighten you up and give you such a good time that you'll quite forget how lonely you have been at Mindaroona. By the way, what are you going to put on for dinner?—we dine at half-past six."

"Oh, anything will do," said Mrs. Hesseltine, still mopping her eyes. "My old black crepe de chine, I suppose."

But Laura Martin was already down on her knees on the floor investigating Mrs. Hesseltine's Saratoga. She had a profound belief in the consoling properties of dress. "No, indeed," she said, "you've got to look your best while you're with me. You must wear this lovely white lace over gold tissue."

Mrs. Hesseltine faintly deprecated the white lace over gold tissue, but her objections quickly waned, and soon she temporarily forgot all her unhappiness in an animated discussion with Laura as to which would go best with the gown, a gold band round her hair or the artistic, but rather severe, Greek knot.

Both finally voted for simplicity and the Greek knot.

Laura left the field victorious, and there was an enigmatic smile on her lips as she met Nelly, the housemaid, in the passage.

"How is Mrs. Robertson getting on in number four, Nelly?" she inquired.

"She's doing very nicely, madam," replied the well-trained maid, with a smile, "and the twins are such splendid, healthy little chaps. One of them has been bawling a good bit this afternoon—he seems to have a terrible temper—but the other is as good as gold. Nurse has got them both out on the back verandah now, if you'd like to see them."

14

But Laura Martin postponed the interview. A wild idea had come into her head, and she wanted to think it out quietly.

The big dining-room at 'The Cedars' was provided with numerous separate tables for the paying guests, and when Mrs. Hesseltine sailed in, rather late, in the wonderful white lace over gold tissue, with her hair done in a Greek knot, she created a mild sensation. Young gentlemen turned their heads and followed her progress with undisguised admiration as she made her way to Mrs. Martin's private table at the far end of the room.

There was much nudging and whispering. A subdued chorus of "Who is she?" went round, and several very plain but expensively dressed ladies looked down their noses and began to talk eagerly to each other about nothing at all. An experienced mind-reader could see by their backs that they were thinking it was a great pity that the young men did not show better taste than to stare at that very conspicuous-looking friend of the proprietress.

Laura congratulated Grace on her improved looks. "My dear," she said, "your frock is perfectly lovely, and the Greek knot is just sweet."

And Grace Hesseltine purred with pleasure. It was much more agreeable, certainly, to dine at this well-ordered establishment, where the paying guests were decidedly presentable and the menu was beyond reproach, than to sit down to a lonely meal with Simon Hesseltine, Esq., of Mindaroona, whose conversation consisted of grumbling at the demands of the Shearers' Union and inveighing against the Government as a gang of robbers.

"Tell me, Grace," said Laura, sipping her claret, "do you ever see anything of the Lintons at Yarralla now? They stayed with me when they came down last year for the Melbourne Cup, just after they were married. He seemed a good sort and she was a very pretty little thing. They are not far from you, are they?"

"Only five miles," said Grace; "I used to drive over fairly often during the winter, to sit and sew with her, although I was horribly envious of her."

"Why on earth should you be envious of her?"

15

"Oh, didn't you know? The stork called at Yarralla about a month ago. Such a dear little girl baby! That was what finally unsettled me, and made me so restless that I simply had to get away from Mindaroona. So I came down to see you."

The older woman's eyes grew wistful for a moment, but she resolutely shook off the weakness. "That's right, dear. I'll see that you have a good time here, and when you go back you'll be a different woman."

"I wonder," said Mrs. Hesseltine. "Do you know, Laura," she continued after a short pause, "I heard a baby crying somewhere upstairs this afternoon, and it brought back all the old pain. I didn't know you accepted people with babies as guests. The poor little things are quite barred at most places nowadays, aren't they?"

Laura Martin sat back in her chair and shot a curious glance at her visitor. "Well," she said, "I wasn't going to tell you about it, but now I suppose I must. My dear, I haven't merely got one baby in this well-regulated establishment—I have two."

"Twins?" ejaculated Mrs. Hesseltine.

"Yes, twin boys," replied Mrs. Martin, "and beautiful babies too, as like each other as two new bright shillings. The mother is a Mrs. Robertson—an Englishwoman, I fancy—who came here a couple of months ago, and I really hadn't the heart to tell her that I couldn't take her in when she told me her story."

"I'm so glad!" said little Mrs. Hesseltine simply.

"To tell you the truth, I was a little bit suspicious about her at first," continued Mrs. Martin, "but I could see that she was a lady, and I was so much impressed by her that at last I let her have the big double room on the second floor. And that's where the twins were born, five weeks ago."

"Oh," ejaculated little Mrs. Hesseltine, "I simply must see them!"

"Mrs. Robertson told me," continued Laura Martin, "that her husband was an officer in some regiment stationed on the Indian frontier—I've really forgotten the outlandish name of the place. Poor thing! she had only been married a couple of months when he was killed in that wretched little expedition against the wild tribes near the Afghan border. You remember there was a lot about it in the newspapers at the time. Of course, his death was a fearful shock to her, and she left India at once. She told me quite frankly that she was very badly off, and that she came to Australia because she thought she could live more cheaply here than in England. Then the twins arrived, and there she is. Goodness knows what she will do now. She has paid up all right so far, but I know she is awfully hard up, poor thing, and I'm quite certain she can't afford to stay here much longer. I was just wondering — —"

"What?" said Mrs. Hesseltine, leaning forward in her chair with her eyes shining.

"I was just wondering where she will go when she leaves 'The Cedars,'" replied Laura Martin, looking at her visitor irresolutely. "It will be so awkward for her, won't it?"

"Do you think — —" began Mrs. Hesseltine tentatively.

"No, I don't — —" snapped Mrs. Martin. "I'm quite certain she wouldn't."

"But I didn't say anything," retorted Grace Hesseltine, opening her eyes wide.

"No. But I know what you were going to say," put in her friend Laura, "and I'm quite certain you oughtn't to tempt her."

"I have more money than I know what to do with," said Mrs. Hesseltine obstinately.

"And no children," said Laura, looking her friend straight in the face.

"Well, she has more children than she knows what to do with, and no money," muttered Mrs. Hesseltine rebelliously. "I don't see why it shouldn't be managed."

"I won't have anything at all to do with it," said Laura Martin. "I'm not going to encourage you in such a mad idea. What do you think Simon would say?"

"I don't care two straws what Simon would say," retorted Mrs. Hesseltine, "and he knows it. Besides, I think he ought to be delighted if I could find a little happiness that way."

"Very well, dear," said Laura nervously, "we'll talk it over afterwards." She knew from experience that paying guests have

17

very long ears. One of the plainest and most expensively dressed of the ladies at the table behind them was obviously putting a terrible strain upon her aural nerves.

As the elegantly gowned little lady from Mindaroona sailed down the long room towards the door accompanied by the stately proprietress, Mr. Sharp, a rising young solicitor, nudged his friend Mr. Call, one of the best known members of the Stock Exchange Club. "Did you watch their faces?" said the astute legal gentleman. "I gather that the little one has just proposed to Laura that they should blow up Parliament House. And Laura would rather like to undertake the job, if she wasn't so scared."

However, the dark plot took definite shape as Grace Hesseltine and her trusted school-friend of early days sipped their coffee in Mrs. Martin's dainty sitting-room.

"Do ask the nurse to bring them in here and let us look at them," said Mrs. Hesseltine, clasping her hands together in excited anticipation.

Laura Martin held out for fully five minutes, but Grace refused to be pacified with promises, and at last, in response to a smiling request from Mrs. Martin, the white-clad nurse undertook to ask Mrs. Robertson if she might show the babies to Mrs. Martin's friend.

"Ask Mrs. Robertson to come too," said Grace Hesseltine.

And so it came about that the tall pale dark-eyed woman left her room on the second floor, attended by the white-aproned nurse with a twin on each arm, and entered Mrs. Martin's cosy little sitting-room, to find the proprietress chatting with a pretty little fluffy-haired woman who was beautifully dressed and evidently knew it.

Laura introduced the pair in an easy, graceful sentence or two.

"Really, Mrs. Robertson, I'm a perfect fool about babies," prattled the little lady from Mindaroona, "and I am just dying to see yours. What a pair of darlings!" She cooed over the twins, who were still in the nurse's arms. The hair of one was a little darker and more curly than that of the other. But with the exception of that small distinction the babies were facsimiles.

"The dark one is Humphry," said Mrs. Robertson, with a rather wan smile, "and the fair one is Harold. But Harold is sure to get darker as he grows older, and there are gleams of gold in Humphry's hair that make me wonder whether he is not going to be as fair as his brother eventually. Do take one of them in your arms, if you would like to, Mrs. Hesseltine."

"Oh, might I really?" chirped Grace delightedly. "I'll be ever so careful." She scrutinised the infants closely. Humphry regarded her with a solemn stare that plainly portended distrust, if not disapproval. Harold gurgled and actually smiled.

After a moment's hesitation Mrs. Hesseltine selected Harold, and the nurse, by one of those movements which to the unskilful resemble legerdemain deftly transferred the infant in its absurdly long petticoats to the eager arms of the baby-worshipper.

Mrs. Robertson dropped much of her chilly reserve and became almost communicative in the pleasant companionship of Grace and Laura. The twins were a common bond of interest, and taking Humphry from the nurse, Mrs. Robertson sat down with him opposite Simon Hesseltine's pretty wife, who crooned contentedly over her borrowed infant.

When the nurse announced that it was bottle time and proceeded to remove Humphry from his mother's arms, the infant signified its disapprobation by bellowing loudly. But Harold accepted every change of guardianship quite calmly.

"It's quite wonderful how different those two babies are in temperament already," said Mrs. Robertson. "I sometimes fancy that Humphry is more like me and that Harold is more like his dead father."

When the tall dark-haired woman had said good-night and had followed the twins to their improvised nursery, Mrs. Hesseltine laid her hand upon her friend's arm with an air of quiet determination. "I simply must have him, Laura," she said, "and you have got to arrange it. You can tell Mrs. Robertson all about Mindaroona. Simon settled it on me at my marriage and I shall leave everything to the boy. If she lets me adopt him he will have a much better chance in life than if she keeps him herself, and the cheque that I shall hand her as a guarantee of my good faith will enable her to maintain herself and the other boy in reasonable comfort until she either marries again or can establish herself in some business that will be a living for her."

With many misgivings Laura Martin opened up the delicate negotiations on the following morning. And it happened that she found the mother of the twins in a very desponding mood. Mrs. Robertson was down to her last ten pounds and had not the faintest notion where the next money was to come from.

"Mrs. Hesseltine is prepared to give you a cheque for L500," said Laura Martin, "as security for the due fulfilment of her promise to bring up the child in every respect as if he were her own son, the sole condition being that you give this written undertaking to make no further claim to the boy. She will cause him to be educated in a manner suitable to his position, and every provision will be made for his welfare, financially and otherwise."

The tall dark-haired woman bowed her head upon her hands. When she raised it again her face was the colour of marble. "Give me the paper," she said, "and I will sign it."

Thus it came about that Mrs. Hesseltine, accompanied by another white-aproned nurse carrying a particularly even-tempered baby, went on board the R.M.S. Merkara at Port Melbourne, bound for Sydney, while Mrs. Robertson, with the remaining twin in her lap at 'The Cedars,' abandoned herself to unrestrained weeping.

But presently the tall dark-haired lady dried her eyes, for she had taken her resolution.

Going to her cabin trunk in the corner of the room, she opened it and took out a small silver box of Indian workmanship, so beautifully made that when it was closed it was difficult to see where the lid and the sides met. The casket appeared to be absolutely air-tight and water-tight.

Unlocking the box with a small silver key, she took out a ring with a little green stone surrounded by brilliants, a heavy gold bangle with an inscription on the inside, and three papers. One was

20

a marriage certificate, the others were separate certificates of the birth of twin sons, Humphry and Harold, whose parents were set down in the documents as Hector McLean and Mildred McLean, formerly of Tilgit, in the North-west Provinces of British India.

The dark-haired lady replaced the precious documents in the silver box and also the ring and bracelet. Then she laid upon the top of the certificates a cheque for L500, signed 'Grace Hesseltine' and payable to bearer. Having done this, she locked the silver casket and put it back in her cabin trunk.

"She shall have her cheque back," said the dark-haired lady through her teeth, "and I will have my child again, agreement or no agreement."

Telling Laura Martin that she was compelled to go away for a few days on business and leaving the infant Humphry with his nurse in the care of the proprietress, the lady who was known as Mrs. Robertson, with her last ten pounds in her purse and her cabin trunk packed with a few necessaries for travelling, called a cab and left 'The Cedars.'

The days went by and the weeks passed. But the woman who was known as Mrs. Robertson returned no more, and all Mrs. Martin's advertisements and inquiries were fruitless.

The mother of the twin babies had vanished as completely as though the solid earth had opened under her feet and then closed over her again.

CHAPTER III

TWENTY YEARS AFTER

Nobody either at headquarters or anywhere else could say definitely why Major McLean resigned from the military forces of the Commonwealth and buried himself on his own little station-property near Blackfish Bay.

On his return from India he had accepted the adjutancy of a mounted infantry regiment. Then on the outbreak of the South African War he had volunteered for active service. He fought bravely throughout the war, and returned with a slight wound and the D.S.O. Soon after his return he sent in his papers and retired to his station, Caringal, a few miles from Blackfish Bay, on the New South Wales coast.

One boundary fence of Caringal ran down to Yarralla, where Mrs. Linton, a widow, lived with her charming daughter Leonie, and another of the major's boundaries just touched Mindaroona, where Mrs. Hesseltine and her son Harold were very companionable neighbours.

It was a delightful spring morning, and the major's forty-third birthday, as he walked across the Mindaroona paddocks to make an early call on Mrs. Hesseltine.

Grace Hesseltine, plumper than of yore but still decidedly attractive, and like all very fair women carrying her years lightly, sat on the verandah of the substantial homestead sewing.

"How early you are this morning, Major," she said with a bright smile as she advanced with outstretched hand. "I suppose you are looking for Harold again."

"Of course I am," replied the major with a frank grin. Since old Simon Hesseltine had departed ten years before for a region where the Shearers' Union could trouble him no more, the major had been a very constant visitor at Mindaroona.

"The boy has gone out for a ride with Leonie Linton," said the attractive widow, resuming her sewing and motioning to her visitor to take the vacant chair beside her. "But they'll be back for lunch. What's the programme for to-day?"

"Well, to tell you the truth," said the major apologetically, "I was going to suggest a little holiday trip. I want to take a run down to the ironworks at Shaleville to see how they are getting on with the new plant there. It occurred to me that you might all like to come with me."

"Oh, how jolly!" said Mrs. Hesseltine delightedly. "We'll take the big car and have afternoon tea out of doors. It will be a regular picnic. You'll stay to lunch here, of course?"

"Thanks awfully," said the major, lighting a cigarette and puffing at it contentedly. The companionship of the gracious woman beside him was very pleasant, and he took a genuine interest in her handsome son, who intended to devote himself to a military career. The major often said to himself that if he had ever had a son he would have wished that son to be just like Harold Hesseltine.

"Here they come," exclaimed Mrs. Hesseltine suddenly, pointing out across the big home paddock, "and racing again, of course."

The major looked and saw two little clouds of dust travelling fast side by side. Presently two figures on horseback emerged and the drumming of hoofs came faintly to the ears of the watchers. Side by side the riders swept along at top speed, and as they pulled up their mounts, laughing and excited, just outside the white paling fence, the major loudly called, "Dead heat!"

Dismounting quickly, Harold helped Leonie to alight, and together the good-looking pair came towards the verandah, as Mike, the rouseabout, led away the steaming horses.

"Miss Linton beat me home by a neck, sir," said Harold, saluting the major, "but there was really nothing between us."

"Wasn't there though?" said Mrs. Hesseltine, with a significant glance at the major. "Well, I'm surprised to hear it."

The flush that flew to Leonie's cheeks was wonderfully becoming. In the excitement of the gallop her fair hair had escaped from under her hat and was flowing over her shoulders. Her eyes were fairly aglow with light. "I believe he pulled the black horse and let me win, Mrs. Hesseltine," she exclaimed; "wasn't it mean of him?"

"Ah, my dear," said the widow, letting her eyes rest affectionately on the tall young fellow beside her, "in Harold's eyes a woman must always be first." And then she whispered to the major, "If the occasion ever arose he would give up everything for a woman. I am sure of that. And I believe you would do the same yourself, major."

But the major did not answer. He was thinking of a certain day twenty years before in India, when he made up his mind to give up everything—his position, his career, his life's work—for a woman, and when she had saved him from the necessity by freeing him voluntarily from the encumbrance of herself. He had never seen her since. Every effort to trace her had failed. He did not even know whether she still lived or not, and the uncertainty had clouded his whole life.

The voice of the frank young fellow, whose face so curiously called up vague fleeting recollections of those dim past days, broke in upon the major's reverie. "What are we going to do to-day, sir?" he asked; "I feel fit for anything."

The major explained his idea of a visit to the ironworks at Shaleville. He would be delighted if Mrs. Hesseltine, Miss Linton, and Harold would accompany him.

The suggestion was received with warm applause, and after lunch the four started off in the big motor-car for Shaleville, the prosperous little town that had sprung up around the great ironworks that had been built over a coal-mine by a long-sighted capitalist of a past generation.

Mrs. Hesseltine and Leonie Linton picked up their skirts and trod daintily as they walked down the main street, and turning in at last through a gate in the high paling fence, entered the area

24

covered by the ironworks. The major walked in front to pilot them and Harold brought up the rear.

The day had turned bitterly cold and there was a feeling of snow in the air, for Shaleville, with its encircling rampart of hills, was nearly 4,000 feet above sea-level.

As the four visitors entered the gate a young workman passed them carrying a bar of iron on his shoulder. He wore a rough brown jersey, moleskin trousers, and heavy boots. His face was so thickly grimed with coaldust that his features were quite indistinguishable. He took in the whole party with one swift glance, and then hurried on in front of them and vanished into the works.

"That's a smart young fellow," said the major to Mr. Blunt, the grizzled old foreman who had been deputed to show the party round. "Born and bred to the work, I suppose."

The old foreman was very deaf, but after the major had shouted the remark in his ear three or four times he began to understand.

"No," said Mr. Blunt; "we get a lot of the lads locally, but as a matter of fact that young chap's a stranger. Comes from t'other side of the Murray, I fancy. He came here looking for a job only last week, an' I put him on at the fishplates—punching holes in 'em, y' know. We'll get down there presently and see 'im at work. These 'ere are the puddling furnaces."

As the visitors stepped into the first huge open shed further conversation became impossible, owing to the roar of the furnaces and the banging of the big steam-hammers.

Leonie clutched Harold's sleeve nervously as the guide halted in front of one of the furnaces where a grimy and perspiring toiler stood puddling the molten metal with a long iron bar.

"Ye needn't be afraid, missy," remarked the guide encouragingly. "It's for all the world like making butter. 'E jest goes ahead churnin' with that there iron bar, and presently the iron forms itself inter a big lump, wot we calls a puddled ball, an' that's the butter. You'll see it come out in a minute."

As he spoke the operator threw the door of the furnace fully open and hooked out a huge glowing cannon ball from the blinding sea of liquid iron. It dropped upon a small trolley and was quickly wheeled by an impish urchin to where a grimy giant clad in armour and with his face protected by a visor stood in front of the steam-hammer. The giant transferred the lump to his anvil and banged and squeezed it with his mighty hammer, while large flakes of fire fell all round him and the molten fiery juice of its impurities dripped from the puddled ball.

"Isn't it terrifying," said Leonie, gripping Harold by the arm and getting a reassuring squeeze of the hand from her protector. "I shouldn't like to think that any one I was fond of had to work in this weird place."

"It's man's work though, isn't it, Leonie?" said Harold, through the roar of the furnaces and the dull thud, thud of the falling hammer. "I can't help admiring a fellow who takes on work like this. It's a bit different from selling ribbons behind a counter, anyhow."

But the foreman was moving on, and they had to follow him, picking their way carefully among the glowing fragments that lay about the ground in every direction.

They saw the puddled ball much reduced in size by the loss of the impurities that had been banged out of it. It was placed in the rolling mill—a series of gigantic mangles differently shaped and grooved, which worked in the centre of a long iron roadway furnished with rapidly revolving rollers.

"Ye see," roared the grizzled guide through the deafening din of the mills, "we puts her in like this,"—he pointed to the red-hot flattened mass of the long-suffering puddled ball, which was just entering upon a further stage of treatment—"and she comes out like that."

The red-hot mass was placed on the iron roadway, where it was speedily caught by the revolving rollers and hurried forward to the ordeal of the monstrous mangle. And as the visitors gazed they saw it transformed under their eyes into a long thin red-hot snake, which shot out from under the mangle and sped along the iron roadway on the other side, to be cut and cooled in due course into convenient lengths of wrought bar-iron.

26

"Oh, what an appalling squeeze!" laughed Mrs. Hesseltine, throwing an arch look at the major. "It positively makes one feel a pang of pity for one's poker, to think that it must have gone through the same ordeal."

"At least, if it wasn't the same ordeal it was another as like it as two p's," retorted the major quizzically, "since that's the happy little letter you are so fond of."

And then he possessed himself of the lady's arm under the pretext of preventing her from slipping into the fatal embraces of the rolling mill. Mrs. Hesseltine did not withdraw her arm. The major was certainly a very satisfying person to be with.

And she caught herself wondering why he did not possess himself of her arm more often, and why, since he obviously admired her, he so seldom allowed himself to overpass the rigid bounds of ordinary acquaintanceship. This was a thought that had often troubled the charming chatelaine of Mindaroona. And it persisted in obtruding itself even in the midst of this noisy din of whirring, clanking, screeching machinery. Why did the major stop short just when her instinct told her that he felt most drawn towards her? He was the most perplexing middle-aged bachelor she had ever met. Most of them wanted to make love to her on sight. And then the widow began to be conscious of a vague apprehension—she could hardly analyse it—concerning the major's early life, which he hardly ever talked about.

All this flashed through her brain as she walked along beside the major, paying no attention whatever to the old foreman in front of them, even when he expatiated on the many merits of the new steel-furnace and pointed out the big ingots of steel that were being reheated and then passed through the rolling-mills, to emerge in the form of red-hot girders, channeling, fishplates and various other kinds of useful hardware that were being sawn into convenient lengths by a methodical buzz-saw, which screeched without intermission over its task.

Mrs. Hesseltine found metal more attractive in her own thoughts—which were mainly about the major—than in the "stupid old iron-works," which were merely useful as a back-ground.

27

Suddenly, just as they paused in front of the punching-machine, which was boring holes in red-hot fishplates under the supervision of the extremely grimy-faced young workman who had passed them near the entrance, Mrs. Hesseltine found herself confronted by a paralysing though unspoken question. It was this: Was there any reason—anything in the major's past life—which prevented him from proposing to her? That he was a bachelor she had always supposed. But after all, what solid justification had she for such a supposition?

As the question flashed through Mrs. Hesseltine's brain, she looked up, and found herself staring straight into the eyes of the young workman, who, according to the foreman, had only recently come to Shaleville from "t'other side of the Murray."

The young workman's gaze was positively disquieting. There seemed to be almost a hint of menace in it. And his face was quite preposterously grimy. It almost looked as though he had blackened it with coaldust on purpose. None of the other workmen were nearly so dirty.

"Oh!" said Mrs. Hesseltine, nervously clutching the major's arm. "That young fellow gave me quite a start."

"There's nothing wrong about him that I can see," whispered the major reassuringly. "A very decent young fellow, I'm sure. Just watch him at his work for a minute."

The party of visitors paused in front of the punching-machine and watched the young workman, who had a boy to assist him. Armed with a big pair of pincers, the man seized a red-hot fishplate, swung it into place, and then pulled a lever which brought down a row of punches that went through the iron as though it was cheese, and dropped the punched out cores on the ground beneath. The boy, who also wielded a pair of pincers, grasped the finished article and stacked it with the others. And so the work proceeded with monotonous iteration, varied only by the occasional jamming of a fishplate in the punching-machine and the consequent necessity of pulling it out again with the pincers and reinserting it straight.

"Really I must get out into the open air," said the widow

abruptly. "The heat and the noise in here have made me feel quite faint." She passed her hand across her forehead with a gesture of weariness that did not escape the notice of the alert major, and he hurried her forward at once.

Leonie ran up to see what was the matter, and taking Mrs. Hesseltine's disengaged arm, helped the major to support her until they emerged from the machinery-shed and stood once more in the open air.

But if the mistress of Mindaroona had looked back she would have seen a very peculiar little incident. She would have seen the preternaturally grimy-faced young workman at the punching-machine desist from his work for a moment to run after Harold, tap him on the back, and thrust a piece of paper into his hand. Then she would have seen the young workman place his finger on his lip with an imperative appeal for silence, and go back to the punching-machine, where an open-mouthed urchin stood gaping at him with a red-hot fishplate in his pincers.

Harold opened the note and read it with a puzzled brow. When he had finished it he crushed it up in his hand, thrust it into his pocket, and ran after the major, Mrs. Hesseltine, and Leonie.

He found them discussing some point of evident importance with Mr. Blunt, the foreman.

"Askin' your pardon, sir," Mr. Blunt was saying to the major, "but your good lady hasn't seen the galvanising bath yet. It's one of the most interesting things we do 'ere an' I'm sure she orter see it before she goes."

"I wish the man wouldn't persist in calling me your good lady, Major," said the widow testily, "and I wouldn't go to see his old galvanising bath for a hundred pounds. I wish he'd go and drown himself in it. I want to get out of this and go home. Can't you explain that I'm feeling ill?"

"Mrs. Hesseltine is not very well to-day," shouted the major desperately, "and she would like to postpone the rest of the inspection until some other day."

Mr. Blunt nodded as though he understood, but it was all a bluff. "Ye see, mum," he continued, demonstrating with lifted

29

forefinger in front of the exasperated widow, "we puts the ingots of spelter—that's lead, tin, and such-like—with a little sal ammoniac inter the galvanising bath. Then we puts in a steel sheet, plain or corrugated, an' out she comes with a beautiful mottled sheen, like wot you 'ave seen, no doubt, on your own station. They calls it galvanised iron, mum—but that's a mistake, if you'll excuse me for saying so. There ain't a square yard of galvanised iron in the country. It's all galvanised steel now, an' very useful too fer making churches, coalsheds, buggy-houses, or any little thing like that about the place."

"For goodness' sake, make him stop, Major." The handsome widow was almost crying by this time.

"If you wouldn't mind showing us the way to the gate, Mr. Blunt," said the major, "we would be extremely obliged to you. We really must be going now."

Mr. Blunt wagged his head comprehendingly and led the way through more machinery. "Would you mind askin' your good lady not to step in that 'ole?" he murmured confidentially, after they had walked about a quarter of a mile; "it's full of 'ot slag. That's the black skin on the top. Very deceptive, that 'ot slag. It come out of the pot that they filled when they tapped the steel-furnace. They drawed off the steel, ye see, into them moulds, and this 'ere slag was left be'ind."

The molten stone bubbled up yellow and fiery through the cracks in the black skin that covered it, and Mrs. Hesseltine trod carefully among the red-hot pitfalls that beset her path. She was desperately tired, her head was aching, and the recollection of the face of the grimy young workman at the punching-machine troubled her seriously.

When Mr. Blunt solemnly produced a pair of blue spectacles and bade her put them on in order that she might gaze unharmed into the dazzling interior of the steel-furnace, Mrs. Hesseltine flatly refused. Indeed, she went on strike. "I-I-I thought you were ta-ta-taking me to the ga-ga-gate," she sobbed to the major; "and I'm simply dying for a cuh-hup-hup of tea."

So the party retreated in good order towards the main gate,

and the major covered the retreat and fought a rearguard action with Mr. Blunt, who displayed prodigious valour in dodging about among pools of burning slag, in his desire to cut off the retirement and compel the visitors to do their duty without shirking.

"My dear, it's very interesting," said Mrs. Hesseltine to Leonie as she dabbed her pretty little nose with something concealed in her lace-edged handkerchief, "but nothing would induce me to go into the place again. Why, it's positively terrifying."

"Yes, but it's beautiful too," said Leonie thoughtfully, with a backward glance towards the dark stalwart figures suddenly bathed in glowing light as a furnace-door was opened, and the cascade of fire that played round the man in armour as he stood before his hammer. "It's the beauty of power and effort and peril—something that we women can see from afar but never take part in."

"My dear Leonie, you're getting quite poetical," said Mrs. Hesseltine. "It's most reassuring. I was beginning to think that you had very little sentiment in your nature. Come along, Harold; we'll be very late getting home as it is."

"I—I'm afraid I'll not be able to go back with you, mother," said Harold hesitatingly. "I have to see a man here, a little later, on particular business."

"Oh, nonsense, my dear boy! What business can you possibly have in the township? Don't be so absurd."

"Really, mother, I must ask you to excuse me just this once. I'll borrow the superintendent's car and get one of the men to drive me home later on in the evening."

"What rubbish, Harold!" said Mrs. Hesseltine testily. "There can be no possible reason why you cannot come home with us now."

Harold fidgeted and reddened, but he remained obstinate. "I'm very sorry, mother," he said finally, "but I really cannot go back with you now."

Mrs. Hesseltine looked sharply at the young fellow and then at the major.

Leonie looked at Harold too. Clearly she was puzzled, but she could no more interpret the boy's refusal to go back to Mindaroona

31

than she could interpret the frowns of Mrs. Hesseltine or the obvious dissatisfaction of the major. All the frank enjoyment of the outing was over, and a vague feeling of mutual distrust descended like a chilly mist upon the party.

Afternoon tea was achieved amid brief banalities, and it was a relief to all when the big motor-car drew up at the side of the main street and took in Mrs. Hesseltine, Leonie, and the major.

"I shall expect you home to-night, Harold," said Mrs. Hesseltine frostily, just before the car drove away; "and please remember that I shall be sitting up for you. You'll be able to borrow the manager's car for the run out. Goodbye."

Leonie gave Harold a chilly nod, and the car sprang forward, leaving Harold standing at the side of the street waving his embarrassed adieux.

The major was gloomy and depressed during the journey home. He found his thoughts recurring first to Harold and then to the woman whom he had married twenty years before, and who had vanished so utterly from his ken. When would that horrible uncertainty be cleared up? His liberty of action was completely fettered by his anxiety.

He fell to wondering whether an important step that he had recently taken would clear up the mystery.

CHAPTER IV

TRACKING THE TRACKER

As Harold turned with mingled feelings of irritation and perplexity to make his way to the Miners' Rest Hotel, he cannoned against an unobtrusively dressed individual who was as deeply wrapped in thought as himself. The stranger's shabby suit suggested the city rather than the Bush, and a hard felt hat that had once been black, but was now green and also greasy at the brim, branded him conclusively as urban and not rural.

"Why the blazes don't you look where you're goin'?" snarled the stranger, who had been pushed off the footpath into the roadway by the impact. Then he glanced up and caught sight of Harold's face. His mouth and eyes opened involuntarily and he stood still, staring at the young fellow with speechless amazement.

"What the devil are you glaring at?" exclaimed Harold, and then he passed on down the street, idly wondering why people who were obviously dotty were allowed to wander about Shaleville at will.

But the stranger kept his eyes fixed on the retreating figure, and presently began to follow Harold.

The shabby individual, still following the young man in front of him, drew from an inner pocket a greasy black notebook stuffed with papers that were confined in place by an elastic band. Among the papers were several cards with the printed inscription, "T. Finegan," and in the right hand lower corner, "Representing Mr. Con Bounce, Private Inquiry Agent, Melbourne."

Searching through the pocket in the cover of the notebook, Mr. Finegan drew out a printed slip with a rude photographic reproduction heading the letterpress.

"It's 'im, sure enough," remarked Mr. Finegan, "an' actin' the toff in style too. Wot a bit er luck! There's fifty of the best hangin' to this as soon as I give the office." He spread out the printed slip and read it once more.

"Humphry Robertson, commonly known as Humphry Martin. Height 5 ft. 11 in. Age 20. Weight about 11 st. 10 lb. Brown eyes, brown curly hair, clear complexion, straight nose, full lips, slight moustache; was last seen wearing blue serge suit and straw hat. Ledger-keeper in Metropolitan Deposit and Mortgage Bank. Wanted for embezzlement. Fifty pounds reward for information leading to arrest and conviction."

"My luck's in all right," continued Finegan. "Good job I happened to see this before I came along on the major's wildgoose chase. I'm on for a double event now, an' if I don't find the missing lady I reckon I'll bag the bank clerk. Won't the D's up at Russell Street chew when Tim Finegan puts in fer the two ponies?" He cackled hideously.

Finegan replaced the paper in his notebook and stowed the book in his inner pocket. "I'll have a drop of schnapps on the strength of it," he murmured. "Fifty thick 'uns, and as easy as kiss yer 'and."

As he turned the next corner, still keeping Harold in view, he almost ran into Sergeant Box.

"Hi, sergeant," he said, "d'ye 'appen to know who that young feller is just ahead of us?"

The sergeant looked down from his superior height on the questioner. "He's a better man than you're ever likely to be," he answered. "That's young Mr. Harold Hesseltine, of Mindaroona."

"Rats!" retorted Finegan angrily. "He's a crook, that's wot 'e is. I knew 'im direckly I laid an eye on 'im."

"You'd better go home an' have a sleep," remarked the constable pityingly. "P'raps you'll be better to-morrow."

But Mr. Finegan was already in full chase. He was determined not to lose sight of his quarry, and with a sensation of relief he saw Harold turn into the 'Miners' Rest' and sit down in the dingy parlour.

After imbibing his schnapps at the bar, he too sat down in the corner, and lit his pipe to assist his reflections on the extraordinary development that had just occurred.

He told himself with a sense of solid satisfaction that the major was a "good mug." He had been paying the private inquiry agent liberal expenses for the last three months and three pounds a week salary to find out what happened to a woman who vanished twenty years before. The major had traced her himself from India to Melbourne, where she had landed from a P. and O. mailboat, but at that point every indication of her movements disappeared. After turning the matter over in his mind incessantly for twenty years, the major had called upon Mr. Con Bounce and explained his requirements. Mr. Bounce was interested and sympathetic, for the major was evidently a man of means, and he readily agreed to an arrangement that 'our Mr. Finegan' should devote his entire attention to the investigation, and that the major should pay a salary of five pounds a week and reasonable expenses to the investigator, who should furnish progress reports of his discoveries. Mr. Bounce's share of the work was to take two pounds a week from Finegan and half the money paid for expenses. As he justly remarked, what was the good of having a business if you made nothing out of it? Then he was able to devote all his own attention to the branch of private inquiry that he had perfected, namely, shepherding broken-down remittance men, and lending them small sums of money for necessary drinks on the security of their reversionary interests in comfortable little properties in the English counties.

Finegan ruminated on the injustice of Fate, which had made him a jackal for Con Bounce instead of the proprietor of that astute individual's valuable business. And then he remarked to himself, "Don't suppose the major'll stand it much longer. And anyhow the fifty thick 'uns will come in handy."

He peeped furtively across the parlour to where Harold sat idly glancing at the Shaleville Intelligencer and looking every two minutes at the clock.

"Good job the major sent for me after all," reflected Mr. Finegan. "It's given me the chance of seeing his nibs over there. I recognised 'im the minute I set eyes on him. He aint altered a bit either since I last saw him when he was living at that swell boarding-house in St. Kilda. My luck's in to-day all right."

And then in a burst of generosity he addressed the young fellow whom he proposed shortly to sell to the police for fifty pounds. "Will you join me in a drink, mate? I'm just goin' to 'ave one."

Harold surveyed his interlocutor slowly from foot to head and then from head to foot again. "No, thanks," he said, and resumed his study of the Shaleville Intelligencer.

"My oath, you're mighty proud, young feller," said Finegan, stung to sudden irritation. "Fer two pins I'd — —-"

But the sentence was never finished, for a stalwart young ironworker, black as a coal and obviously dangerous, opened the door just behind Mr. Finegan and with his powerful shoulder administered a bump to the babbler that sent him staggering halfway across the floor. "Get out of this," remarked the new-comer curtly. "I want to talk to this gentleman."

Mr. Finegan slunk outside muttering to himself, and the young ironworker slammed the door and locked it.

He remained silent for a few seconds, and then suddenly opening the door, found Finegan on his knees outside listening at the keyhole. As Finegan scrambled to his feet and began to run, a vigorous kick, planted exactly in the right place, sent him flying down the passage and into the street, holding the part affected with both his hands and yelling incoherent menaces.

But the newcomer paid no attention whatever to the parting guest whom he had sped so unceremoniously. "I know that rat," he remarked to Harold, whose face he examined intently. "I have seen him in Melbourne and I fancy that it would be very unhealthy for me if he were to recognise me. Tim Finegan would sell his own mother for a plug of tobacco."

"Never mind that loafer," said Harold, whose heart was beating strangely. "What did you mean by the note you gave me this afternoon? My mother was quite upset when I wouldn't go home with her. Good God, man, don't look at me like that!"

36

Humphry stared at Harold in amazement. "Haven't you been told either?" he questioned blankly. And then he muttered under his breath, "The same way that they treated me—the same way exactly."

"Told what?" asked Harold, with a cold foreboding that the anchors of his life were being dragged from their safe holding-ground and that he was drifting, drifting, he knew not whence or whither.

Humphry stepped forward facing Harold, and placing one hand on each of Harold's shoulders, stared the young man straight in the eyes. Humphrey's face was thickly grimed with coaldust still, but his features were strangely, marvellously familiar to Harold.

The young man who had never had the faintest reason to doubt that he was Simon Hesseltine's son found himself scrutinising—his own face.

He turned sick and cold with the shock of the discovery. "What—what does it all mean?" he asked, groping blindly for a chair, and sinking back into it just in time to escape falling on the floor.

"It means that the lady who was with you this afternoon is not your mother," said Humphry huskily, "and that her husband, who died when you were five years old and whom you probably remember quite well, was not your father."

Harold turned faint. His little world was falling about his ears.

"It also means," continued Humphry, "that the woman who brought me up from childhood was not my mother, and that her dead husband was not my father. She admitted it to me last week just before I left Melbourne for ever. She said that she was going to tell me on my twenty-first birthday, but that my disgrace compelled her to make the disclosure earlier."

"What disgrace?" asked Harold.

"I've gone a mucker, that's all," replied Humphry curtly. "I'll tell you about it some day, because—because you are my brother."

Harold started to his feet and held out his hand at the sudden call of kinship. "I knew it," he cried. "I felt it in my bones." He

37

clasped the extended hand of the young coal-begrimed worker and wrung it warmly. "And whatever you have done," he added with fervour, "I am quite sure that it was nothing disgraceful. But would you mind telling me who I am, if I am not Harold Hesseltine, and who you are yourself?"

"I must answer the second question first," said the young fellow, sitting down opposite Harold and resting an elbow on the table. "Mrs. Martin, who brought me up from childhood and who has always been more than kind to me, told me last week, when the police were knocking at the door to arrest me for embezzlement, that my mother had left me in her charge twenty years ago and had then disappeared. She called herself Mrs. Robertson, but Mrs. Martin believed it was not her real name. She left the house one afternoon, with nothing but a small handbag, saying that she would be back in a week, and from that day to this she has never been seen again. Mrs. Martin, who was a childless widow, took care of me and brought me up."

"But who am I?" said Harold with a quivering lip. "Was I deserted too?"

"Mrs. Martin had a great friend named Mrs. Hesseltine," continued Humphry in a hard dry voice, "and Mrs. Hesseltine had no children of her own. The childless woman asked our mother to hand over one of her twin baby boys, promising to adopt him. Mrs. Hesseltine offered our mother money—a large sum of money. Our mother was very poor. She was faced with starvation. She took the childless woman's cheque and she handed to her in exchange—you. Next day she vanished from the face of the earth, and every effort to find her has been fruitless. But the childless woman's cheque has never been presented at the bank. Mrs. Martin says that our mother is dead, but how she died, or where, or who she was, are questions that I am not able to answer. But I shall be able to answer them some day. All that I know is that my name is Humphry Robertson for the present, and that your name is Harold Robertson. When I find how and where our mother died I shall find what was her real name and why—and why she—left me. I know in my heart that she meant to go back to me and I want to find the proof." He leaned his arms upon the table and covered his face in silence.

After a few seconds had elapsed Harold spoke again. "I wonder what our mother's face was like," he whispered.

Humphry put his hand inside his pocket and drew out an old photograph in a new folding pocket-case of brown leather. He opened the case and spread it flat on the table.

"That is our mother," he said. "Mrs. Martin gave me the photograph, which was left behind on the mantelpiece when our mother went away."

The two young men pored over the face in the photograph—a beautiful face, but over-spread by an abiding sadness. It was the face of a woman who had loved and suffered. But it was essentially a strong face, the face of a woman capable of great deeds, whether of good or evil—perhaps of both. In their features the two young men who sat in the dingy bar parlour marvellously resembled the face of the photograph. But the characteristic expression of force either for good or evil in the pictured face was reproduced by only one of them. It was Humphry who was indeed his mother's son.

"You haven't told me yet why you left Melbourne and came to Shaleville," said Harold.

"I must go back a bit first," said Humphry, "or you wouldn't understand. Mrs. Martin was very kind to me. I believe she really loved me. She sent me to a good school and I got on very well. I was in the football team and in the cricket eleven. I did well at my books. Then my mother, as I always thought she was, persuaded me to take a billet in a bank. She knew the manager and I was to get eighty pounds a year. She spoke of it as if it was a wonderful chance. And I was fool enough to take the post. I was there only three months when a warrant was issued for my arrest on a charge of embezzlement. I didn't take the money. Another young fellow took it and lost it at the races. He had not long been married. He got into difficulties and tried to recover himself on the Caulfield Cup. He failed, and he told me that it would break his wife's heart if he was arrested for the theft. I had no wife. I disappeared from the bank, and when the money was missed they jumped to the conclusion that it was I who had taken it. I guessed they would. I escaped when the police were close at my heels, and just before I cleared out Mrs. Martin told me the true story of my birth. I rode my bicycle to Albury, left the machine in the cloak-room, came on to Sydney by rail, and walked from Sydney to Shaleville. I got here a fortnight ago."

"Good Lord!" said Harold in a whisper.

"But, strangely enough," continued Humphry, "a new complication has arisen since I saw you this afternoon at the works. You are so exactly like what I was before I amassed all this dirt that Finegan has identified you as the missing bank clerk, and intends to sell you to the traps. I could see it in his eye when I came into this room, and it's just what I should expect of him. But there is one reason why I cannot allow Finegan to take me."

"And that is?"

"Because I have to clear up the mystery of our mother's disappearance. I intend to find her, Harold, alive or dead."

There was a sombre glow in the eyes of the young man as he stared at his new-found brother, and muttered under his breath again, "Alive or dead."

"By Heaven, I'm with you!" said Harold, who was white and shaken. And then he leaned his head on his hands and said in one great sob, "My mother!"

"I have a feeling in my bones," said Humphry, "that I am on the right track at last and that she is not so very far away now. I shall find her in the end, if Finegan does not sell me to the police and have me sent back to Victoria. After to-night I shall leave the works and take to the Bush again, and perhaps you can help me there."

Harold stood up and clasped his brother's hand. "You can trust me," he said. "And as for Finegan, I fancy he'll find some difficulty in identifying me with the missing bank clerk, but the trouble is that in the course of his rotten inquiries he'll probably bump up against you."

"I wish to goodness he'd break his neck!" said Humphry savagely. "If he is over here foxing after me he may interfere with

40

the great work to which I have devoted myself. But it will be the worse for him if he crosses my path in earnest." A fierce light glowed in the man's eyes, and he brought his clenched fist down on the table with a bang that portended trouble for Finegan if he ever fell into his hands.

Harold gave a slight shudder. There were moments when this new-found brother radiated an impression of terrific force held in very doubtful control. He had a feeling that Humphry would stop at nothing in carrying out the fixed purpose of his heart.

"Now, Harold, we understand each other, don't we?" said Humphry. "I'm here to find the traces of our vanished mother. I'm convinced in my own mind that Mindaroona was connected in some way with the secret of her disappearance. You had been taken there, remember. Mrs. Hesseltine gave a cheque for L500 to our mother as a guarantee of her good faith, and that cheque has never been presented. I have lain awake night after night trying to think out the maddening puzzle, and the only supposition that I can frame to meet all the facts is that our mother was on her way to Mindaroona to recapture you from Mrs. Hesseltine when she met with her fate. Either that or else— — —"

"Or else what?" ejaculated Harold, whose heart was thumping like a trip-hammer.

"Or else this Mrs. Hesseltine knows something about the mystery," said Humphry slowly. "Suppose that our mother arrived at Mindaroona. Suppose that she demanded the return of her baby. Suppose that the demand was refused, and that she was confronted with her written agreement to give the child up altogether. Suppose that a scene ensued between the mother robbed of her son and the childless wife who had obtained that son by playing upon the despair of a woman faced with starvation. I cannot carry my supposition further. All that I know is that our mother vanished from sight from the day that she left 'The Cedars.' And I ask myself in perplexity, 'What does Mrs. Hesseltine know about it?' Is she in any way responsible for that disappearance?"

"Good God! Humphry, what do you mean?"

"I cannot say more. I hardly know what I mean. But I have

come to Shaleville to find out, because it is in easy reach of Mindaroona and because I want to watch this woman who— —"

"Who has adopted me as her son," said Harold bitterly, "and who has given me her love. Oh! Humphry, can't you see how horrible your suspicions are? Until this dreadful mystery is cleared up I can never be happy again."

Humphry was silent for a few moments.

"I cannot help it," he said at last; "but no matter where the search leads me, nor what actions it forces upon me, nor what discoveries I may make in prosecuting it, I intend to go through with it—yes, even if it is to cost me my life—and God help the man who stands in my way. Now I must go. Goodbye, Harold. Go back to Mindaroona, but say nothing of me. I will see you again, and perhaps soon."

"Where are you going to now?"

"I am due at the blast furnace to go on shift at 8 o'clock. We are to tap her at nine, and I cannot be absent. I have a feeling that great things are impending to-night."

Harold shook his brother's hand silently, and left the 'Miners' Rest' to drive back across the ranges to Mindaroona near the sea. Snow was falling on the mountains. He felt chilled to the heart.

CHAPTER V

ON THE TOP OF THE BLAST FURNACE

Tim Finegan had not wasted time after his abrupt departure from the 'Miners' Rest.' Peering through the keyhole before his disconcerting detection by Humphry, he had discovered the extraordinary resemblance between the young workman and the young squatter from Mindaroona. "It's a rum go," muttered Finegan. "They're the dead spit of each other."

And then he saw the solution of the puzzle in a flash. "The ironworker's my man," he ejaculated with conviction, "not the young toff from the station. There's more in this than wot appears at present, but anyhow the ironworker's the bloke wot's wanted for the embezzlement. If I don't get him to-night he'll do the disappearing trick for certain, for I'm sure he recognised me."

Mr. Finegan then proceeded to make inquiries. He soon ascertained that Humphry Robertson, who had changed his name to Scott for reasons best known to himself, was due at the blast furnace at 8 o'clock that evening, having been placed on the shift as an emergency man in consequence of an accident to one of the regular hands. Finegan decided to lie in wait at the blast furnace himself and grab his man there. The reward of 'fifty thick uns' was not to be lightly thrown away, and Finegan's experience told him that the average criminal usually 'turned it up' when tackled by his natural enemy. He did not look forward to the job certainly, but he had thought out a plan for taking his quarry unawares, and he intended to hand him over to Sergeant Box for safe keeping. It was a bit irregular, of course, but Mr. Finegan was not in the habit of shirking irregularities in the course of business, and the scruples would have to be heavy indeed to weigh down fifty thick uns.

A mile away from the township rose the great blast furnace, which was kept going day and night through weekdays Sundays, and holidays, month after month and year after year, smelting the crude ore into pig-iron, to be worked up by other processes into the articles that civilisation inexorably demands. Mr. Finegan turned up his coat-collar round his ears and accompanied Bill Blunt, the foreman, whose favour he had judiciously cultivated through the medium of beer.

"Goin' ter 'ave a fall er snow, I judge," remarked Mr. Blunt, gazing abstractedly at the feathery flakes that were falling all round them. "It gen'ally do snow a bit in July in Shaleville. Ever bin 'ere before?"

Finegan's teeth were chattering. He had never seen snow before. He wished himself back in the cosy corner of his favourite Swanston Street pub in Melbourne. The snow struck him as monstrous, unheard-of, un-Australian. He was quite unaware that it was a familiar sight to every dweller in the mountains. He admitted that he had never been in Shaleville before.

Bill Blunt grunted and piloted the way through sundry mounds of slag, and past an enormous dam full of water, to the blast furnace.

As they approached it the blackness of the sky was illumined at intervals by a sheet of fire that spirted up a hundred feet or more from the top of the furnace and then disappeared entirely, as though a volcano were suddenly put out by an enormous extinguisher.

Presently a broad glare was thrown upon the dark curtain of the night close to the level of the ground. Finegan began to wish that he hadn't come. There was something uncanny about it all. "What's that?" he shouted into Ben Blunt's most serviceable ear.

"They're drorin' off the slag," explained the veteran, pointing to a brilliant golden rivulet that came into view as they turned the last corner. The rivulet ran through a channel in a vast sloping bed of sand. The channel made a sharp right-handed turn and emptied the glowing stream into a huge tank mounted on a railway truck. A locomotive was coupled to the truck and the driver and fireman were nonchalantly preparing for their journey to the slag heap a mile away. This lake of liquid fire was to be hauled to the dumping-

44

ground. Then the truck would be tipped up and the contents shot out upon the flanks of the ever-rising mountain of slag.

"What would happen if the engine left the rails or ran into anything on the way?" yelled Finegan into Blunt's best ear.

"The tankful of molten stuff would be emptied on top of the loco," said Mr. Blunt, stamping his feet to keep himself warm, "and that would be the end of the driver and fireman. Parson 'ud have to read the funeral service over the slag heap, I reckon. You can't come in 'ere, mister, without takin' a bit er resk, ye know."

Finegan began more than ever to wish that he had not come. These men who strode about in rough jerseys and trousers, paddling with great shovels and bars of iron in the seething molten mass to break up the heavy crust that gathered even while it ran, pursued their tasks with stolid unimaginative sang-froid. But the sight of this river of molten stone, flowing out apparently interminably, and the continuous roar of the blast as it entered the furnace, shook the nerve of the private inquiry agent.

He shrank from the task of grappling with the muscular young ironworker in such alarming surroundings. Nothing but the thought of the 'fifty thick uns' sustained him and gave him heart to accompany Bill Blunt to the platform on the top of the blast furnace where he was to see the young fellow who called himself Scott and formally hand him over to Sergeant Box, who had arranged to be in attendance.

Finegan was convinced that to postpone the arrest would be to lose the prisoner altogether. He felt certain that Robertson, alias Scott, had recognised him, had suspected his intention, and would take to the Bush next day, in which case the fifty pounds reward would fall into other and less deserving hands. But the man had been notified to be on the 8 o'clock shift at the blast furnace that night and had said, according to Bill Blunt, that he would be there.

"I 'spose he's a partickler friend of yours, this young chap Scott," volunteered Mr. Blunt as he led the way past the engine-house and into an enormous lift-shaft at the rear of the furnace. "Ye seem mighty set on seein' 'im ter-night."

45

"'Im and me both comes from Melbourne," said Finegan glibly. "We're well acquainted over there, an' bein' in the neighbourhood, I specially want ter see 'im."

"'Ullo, sergeant," ejaculated Mr. Blunt with unfeigned surprise, "wot might you be doin' here?"

"Just come to admire the view, Bill," returned the sergeant, and then he added in an undertone to Finegan, "Remember, 'tis you that's taking the responsibility. Of course, if you identify this young chap as the man that's wanted for the embezzlement and you give him in charge, I'll take him right enough. But it'll be at your risk."

Bill Blunt and Finegan, accompanied by Sergeant Box, entered the great open elevator by which the ore, fluxes, and fuel were carried up to the top of the furnace. Snow was falling heavily by this time, and the hand-trucks full of ore, coke, and limestone were whitened with it as the workmen wheeled them in upon the iron floor of the elevator along with the three passengers. A signal bell rang somewhere, and Finegan held his breath as the elevator moved up with its heavy burden through pitchy darkness to the accompaniment of weird sounds of creaking and clanking.

The roar of the hot-air blast as it rushed into the 'tuyeres' of the furnace beat upon his ears, and he could not even see the outline of his companions.

At last they reached the top and stepped out upon a broad iron platform more than one hundred feet above the ground. Far below them, dimly seen by the light of a few scattered electric lamps, men were putting the final touches to the rows upon rows of moulds in the broad sloping sand-bed destined to receive the molten metal. These were the 'pigs' and the broader transverse channels from which they were fed were the 'sows.' The workers below were armed with shovels and iron bars.

Finegan looked anxiously over. "Our man isn't there," he said to Sergeant Box. "I have information that he is to be on duty up here at 9 o'clock. You'd better stand back in the shadow until I call you, and then, as soon as I find that it's 'im all right and no risk of a mistake, you just grab 'im and slip the irons on 'im. He's a tough-lookin' customer and we don't want no fightin' up here."

Sergeant Box stepped back into the shadow fingering his handcuffs and Finegan walked forward nervously with Bill Blunt towards the front part of the platform, where a thin sheet of iron formed a screen dividing the main platform from the shallow saucer-shaped top of the furnace, in the centre of which was a big black cone operated by a lever, which was worked by a man behind the iron screen.

The saucer-shaped top of the furnace was replenished from time to time by men who emptied into it big wheelbarrowfuls of ore, limestone, and coke that had been brought up by the elevator. This was a continuous process, and at intervals the man behind the screen worked his lever, which lowered the cone and allowed the collected material to slide down into the furnace in such a way that by striking against the cone it was evenly distributed all round.

Every time that the cone was lowered, making an orifice in the top of the furnace, a great sheet of ruddy flame shot up to a terrific height, illuminating the surrounding scene, throwing up the detail of every chimney and building and silhouetting the faces of the workmen with extraordinary distinctness.

Bill Blunt went forward and relieved the man who was in charge of the lever operating the cone. The night had set in bitterly cold and the snow was already lying an inch thick on the iron platform.

"Wish to blazes he'd 'urry up!" muttered Finegan, looking down to the ground to see if he could distinguish the figure of the man who called himself Scott, but who was really Humphry Robertson according to Mr. Finegan's firm conviction. "This 'orrible place gives me the fair 'ump."

He walked forward and watched the men methodically depositing their barrow-loads of material in the saucer-shaped top of the furnace, made of sheet steel lined with fire-brick. The great circular saucer with the cone in place in the middle was nearly full. Finegan looked at his watch. It was five minutes to nine.

"You're sure that the young chap Scott will be up here at nine?" he shouted anxiously to Bill Blunt.

"Dunno about that," replied Mr. Blunt, scratching his head.

47

"Shouldn't wonder if Morton wants him down below while they're tapping, but he'll be up here d'reckly arter, anyhow."

Finegan's jaw dropped. He wanted to get the business over and he had an intense desire to get away from this terrifying furnace that vomited forth rivers of molten rock and metal at the bidding of these cool, unperturbed, blackavised toilers who controlled it.

"There's your man!" ejaculated Bill Blunt, pointing to a worker far below who was poling along the coagulations of the molten slag in the stream that ran through its channel in the sand to the tank on the truck attached to the locomotive in the siding.

Finegan looked down, and by the brilliant glare from the molten slag he saw the face of the young fellow whom he had met that afternoon at the Miners' Rest. Humphry had had a wash since then, and his features were now perfectly distinguishable.

The private inquiry agent took his note-book from his pocket and extracted the newspaper cutting and the printed portrait of the wanted man. He compared the portrait with the face that he saw below him—every line and contour revealed by the dazzling light from the molten stream. There could no longer be the faintest doubt in his mind that Scott was indeed Humphry Robertson. He replaced the note-book in his pocket and fastened his eyes on the worker far below, who was unconscious of the scrutiny.

"Any danger to the men while they're drorin' off the metal?" he inquired carelessly of Bill Blunt. He would not let himself think of the painful possibility that the wanted man might be killed by an accident before he, Finegan, could draw the reward for putting him away.

"Well, not exackly wot you might call danger," remarked Bill Blunt oracularly, "but of course there's always a bit of a resk."

Finegan was not in the mood for drawing such fine distinctions. He demanded explicitness. "Wot could 'appen to 'em, anyway?" he inquired nervously.

"Well," shouted Mr. Blunt, for the roar of the blast that whirled through the tuyeres made conversation a trifle difficult, "in the first place the 'sows' 'ave a way of bilin' over occasionally an' squirtin' 'arf a 'undredweight or so of molten metal over anybody wots 'andy; or then, again, there might be a blow-out when they're drorin off the stuff from the furnace. But old 'ard, they're goin' to tap 'er now."

Finegan went back chafing with nervous anxiety. He fervently hoped that the sows would not boil over upon Scott, alias Robertson, and that there would be no blow-out to do him damage until the fifty pounds was handed over for delivering the prisoner safe and sound into the custody of the law.

Down below half a dozen men, including Humphry Robertson, made ready to tap the bath in which the molten metal collected at the bottom of the furnace. There would be thirty or forty tons of the stuff to come out.

They took a long iron bar with a sharp point to it and attacked the plug of fireclay in the side of the furnace with it, using the bar as a battering ram. Thud, thud, thump, went the bar, and the fireclay, baked as hard as porcelain, gave forth a hollow ringing sound.

All at once the point of the bar went through and a jet of bright golden liquid leaped out in a perfect arch and fell into the channel cut in the sand to receive it. The men started back into safety and the stream rushed along down the main channel, filling all the subsidiary channels, the 'sows' and 'pigs,' that spread out in the pattern of a huge gridiron upon the big sand-bed.

Finegan walked up and down in a frenzy of agitation on the high platform on top of the furnace. He heartily wished that this dangerous business was over. He had no eye for the picturesqueness of the scene, and yet its weird beauty might well have riveted the attention of any one less absorbed in his own plots than the private inquiry agent.

As he stepped back to the rear of the platform Bill Blunt pulled over the lever that operated the cone which closed the opening in the top of the furnace. A great column of flame shot up into the night, blown to this side and that by the force of the rising wind. The flame was parti-coloured, owing to the gases liberated from the melting ore, and it soared aloft in mighty standards that changed from green to rose-pink and then to gold and purple against the dark back-ground of the sky.

All around the floating banners of fire fell the snowflakes, white and silent, encircling the many-coloured sheets of flame.

Rising flames and falling snow. It was the sight that the French soldiers saw at Moscow—the sight that portended their destruction.

It lasted for a minute or two, and then Bill Blunt raised the cone again and closed the furnace, for the saucer-shaped cover was empty. The ore, coke, and limestone had all slid slowly down to the central opening and been evenly distributed by impact with the sides of the cone into the heart of the seething sea of fire beneath.

Finegan trembled and it was not with the cold. He moved back a few yards further away from the receptacle for the ore and fuel. His mottled complexion had become a dirty green. "Wish I was outer this 'ell of a place and 'ome in Footscray," he muttered.

He had no eyes for the strangely impressive scene—the distant fire of the puddling furnace on one side and the red glare from the replenished slag-mountain on the other, the tall black chimneys spouting flame, and down on the great sloping sand-bed immediately below him the delicate tracery of the golden molten iron patterned in the sand moulds, like a great piece of jewellery made by the cunning hand of a giant artificer.

Red glare of fire, inky blackness of the tall chimneys, and over all and through all, lit up by the many-coloured flames, the white unsullied beauty of the falling snow!

"Blast this 'ole of a place," muttered Mr. Finegan hoarsely; "wish I 'adn't 'ave come."

He heard a creaking, clanking noise through the roar of the hot air in the tuyeres, and the elevator stopped almost beside him. Out of it came a loaded barrowful of ore, which was wheeled forward by a sturdy young fellow, so intent on his work that he noticed neither the stranger who stood near with the collar of his heavy overcoat turned up round his ears nor the constable in helmet and water-proofs who stood back in the shadow.

Finegan made a rapid gesture to Sergeant Box, motioning to

him not to show himself, and then he followed Humphry Robertson forward to the receptacle for the ore and fuel immediately above the furnace.

The young fellow tilted his barrowful of ore into the saucer-shaped receptacle. The reservoir was full.

Bill Blunt looked out from behind his screen, saw that the mingled mass of ore, fuel, and flux was up to the level of the platform, and reached for the lever operating the cone.

It was precisely at that moment that Finegan, who had screwed his courage to the sticking-point, stepped forward and laid his hand on the young workman's shoulder. "Humphry Robertson," he said, "you're wanted for embezzlement. Sergeant Box is here and you had better come quietly."

The young man turned round quickly. He was half dazed for a moment. He took a step forward, which had the effect of placing Finegan between him and the ore-holder.

Next instant he caught sight of Finegan's face and recognised him.

"You cur!" he said. And with the words he shot out a lightning-like blow that caught the hapless private inquiry agent flush on the mouth.

Finegan reeled, tottered, lost his balance, stepped backward, and fell over into the saucer-shaped ore-holder above the furnace.

The whole incident had passed in a few seconds, and it was unseen by Bill Blunt on the other side of his iron screen. Furthermore, Mr. Blunt, being woefully deaf, did not hear the piercing scream of Finegan as the central cone began to descend, and the flame from the furnace leaped up with the roar of a liberated demon—not thirty feet distant from him.

The ore, coke, and limestone began to slide slowly down towards the central opening which appeared when the cone was lowered.

Finegan began to slide down also. He scrabbled furiously to regain the edge of the reservoir. In the furnace below the cone was a raging white-hot sea of molten rock and metal.

The lumps of coke and stone slipped away under his frantic

feet and clawing hands; he was being carried quickly to the opening.

Suddenly he felt himself clutched by the collar.

Humphry Robertson had leaped into the ore-holder after him, and was striving to drag him up to safety. But still the stuff slipped away under them down the inclined surface towards the opening into the furnace, from which a sheet of parti-coloured fire was leaping a hundred feet into the air.

The screams of the despairing Finegan were unheard above the roar of the flame, and Bill Blunt, with his hand still on the lever, knew nothing of the awful predicament of the two men in the ore-holder. He might have raised the cone and saved them if he had known.

Humphry Robertson fought hard for two lives down in that terrible death-trap. He was young and powerful, and as lithe as a cat. Unhampered by Finegan he could have scrambled out himself, yet his hand gripped tight on the man's collar, and for a few seconds he held his position against the sliding mass of material. He realised that a few seconds more must end the struggle unless help came.

Suddenly he felt something hard thrust under his left arm. He looked up and saw Sergeant Box on the edge of the platform holding out a long, stout iron bar. Humphry supported his weight upon it, still clutching Finegan by the collar. The heat from the escaping pillar of fire was intolerable. The glare was blinding. The inert deadweight of the burden that Humphry grasped showed him that Finegan was unconscious.

A bell clanged furiously somewhere.

The blast was shut off and the leaping pillar of flame descended into the furnace again.

Then at last Mr. Blunt discovered that something was wrong and raised the cone. The mass of ore and fuel ceased to slip away under the feet of the two men.

Humphry Robertson, still supported by the welcome iron bar, gradually levered himself up towards the edge of the platform, dragging Finegan after him by the collar. In another couple of seconds Sergeant Box grasped Humphry's arm and hauled him out of the ore-holder, still clasping Finegan tightly by the coat-collar.

"By God, you're a man!" said Sergeant Box, and he slapped the young workman on the shoulder with his leg-of-mutton fist.

Together they lifted the unconscious form of Finegan and carried him into a little cubby-house on the roof where the men were accustomed to make their tea and eat their suppers. They laid him on a narrow bench and Sergeant Box dashed cold water in his face. Finegan came to his senses and stared wildly round him. Then he burst into tears.

"Reckon he's had the shock of his life," said Sergeant Box. "It's a good job I was watching you, my lad, or you and he would be pig iron by now. I was only just in time with that iron bar."

Humphry looked straight into the sergeant's face. "Well, are you going to take me now?" he asked.

"Not me," said the sergeant. "I know nothing about you, except that you are a brave man."

He took hold of Finegan by the arm and shook him. The smoky oil lamp threw dancing shadows on the wall of the cubby-house.

"See here, Finegan," said the sergeant, "do you wish to identify this young fellow as a man who's wanted by the police in Victoria?"

Finegan shook his head feebly, "I reckon—I must 'ave—made—a mistake," he muttered under his breath.

So Sergeant Box went home empty-handed after all, and it was a terribly shaken private inquiry agent who crawled back to his bed in Shaleville, leaving Humphry Robertson at work among the fires and the falling snow, rejoicing that he was still free to carry on the great quest.

CHAPTER VI

THE MAJOR ON THE TRAIL

Mrs. Linton was one of those charming middle-aged ladies who always like to have plenty of young people round them, and accordingly, when Leonie rested her fresh young face against her mother's cheek with a whispered petition that she might invite her great friend Marion Bingham up to Yarralla for a visit, Mrs. Linton promptly said that it was a delightful idea.

"Go and write to her at once, dear," said Mrs. Linton. "It is extraordinary how I miss that girl whenever she leaves us. There is something so genuine and trustworthy about her, and I'm sure she will do you good. You have not been looking quite yourself, dear, lately, and I am just beginning to feel a little worried about you."

And indeed Leonie was not nearly as bright as she used to be. She had never been quite the same since that trip to Shaleville, and Mrs. Linton, who was an observant mother, made up her mind that the young lovers had had some misunderstanding.

The truth of the matter was that Harold was quite changed after the visit to the iron-works. Instead of the gay lighthearted boy that she used to know, Leonie found herself trying to talk to a moody introspective youth, who appeared to have on his mind some gloomy secret which he resolutely refused to share with her.

Moreover, he avoided even his mother as far as possible and Mrs. Hesseltine seemed to be almost frightened by his manner towards her. He wore the air of a mute questioner of Fate—and her. She bitterly regretted that she had never told him the true story of his parentage. But it seemed too late now. An atmosphere of suspicion and uneasiness settled down over Mindaroona, a cloud of coolness and perplexity gathered between Mindaroona and the Lintons' place, Yarralla, while even the major, alone with his old housekeeper at Caringal, felt himself separated from his neighbours by a mist of vague misunderstanding.

The major's perplexity increased when he traced the whole trouble back to that visit to Shaleville and the meeting with that mysterious young workman whose presence had so strangely disquieted Mrs. Hesseltine.

The following week brought several new visitors to the district.

Marion Bingham came up from Sydney to stay with Leonie and Mrs. Linton at Yarralla, bringing with her a pleasant whiff of metropolitan life and also a quiet sense of restfulness and power. Intellect and feeling were perfectly balanced in Marion, and brain and sympathy with her worked hand in hand.

"I don't know how it is, my dear," said Mrs. Linton, clasping Marion's hand on the evening of her arrival, "but you always make me feel that life's little worries cannot exist in your presence. They become simply impertinent intruders."

On the same evening, by coach from Shaleville, arrived Mr. Tim Finegan, bound for Caringal in response to an imperative summons from Major McLean. The major expressed a strong desire to know the result of Mr. Finegan's prolonged and highly-paid inquiries upon the subject of the disappearance of 'Mrs. Harrington' whom he had traced to Melbourne from India, but who had vanished utterly just twenty years earlier. Was she alive or dead? The uncertainty was making the major old and irritable before his time. He had loved his wife very truly, but the tragedy of their brief married life lay far in the past, and nothing remained to remind him of it except his thoughts.

Mrs. Hesseltine had attracted him strongly, and he was painfully conscious of the perplexing and ambiguous attitude that he had been obliged to adopt towards her. If only Finegan could clear up the mystery of his wife's disappearance the perplexity would vanish at once and the situation might soon be regularised.

The major smiled contentedly and blew rings with his cigar smoke as he lay on his verandah in a long deck-chair, thinking of how he would regularise the situation. Meantime, what the deuce was keeping Finegan?

As the major reclined in his chair, still thinking of Mrs. Hesseltine's blue eyes and charming figure, the buggy that he had sent to meet the coach drew up at the fence and Finegan got out, obviously nervous and uncomfortable.

His verbal report to the major on the verandah was long-winded and discursive. The major listened with increasing signs of impatience.

"But hang it all, Finegan," said the major at last, "you have found out nothing. You haven't even discovered where Mrs. Harrington lived while she was in Melbourne. I don't want to hear all that stuff about the cabman and the baggage agent and the hall-porter at the Grand Hotel. Accepting your version, it simply amounts to this—that a lady who may or may not have been Mrs. Harrington, but who called herself Mrs. Robertson and whose baggage was labelled with that name, joined the Merovia at Colombo and travelled by that boat to Melbourne, where she disembarked, drove in a cab to the Grand Hotel, had two trunks and a dressing-case delivered to her there by the regular baggage agents, and left with her trunks two days later in a cab. Now, where did she drive to? When you have found that out we shall be one stage nearer to the goal of discovering what became of her eventually."

"Nice game to try and find out where a lady drove to from the Grand Hotel twenty years ago, ain't it?"

"Find the cabman."

"Can't do it, major. Most of the old ones have left the job on account of them taxicabs. Besides, what cabman could remember where he drove a particular fare twenty years ago?"

Mr. Finegan was suspicious of the major. He disliked this vigorous method of pushing inquiries. It might conceivably produce definite results. And definite results meant that a lucrative job might be brought to an end. Amateurs, in Mr. Finegan's opinion, had no right to interfere when they engaged a professional investigator. Their business was to receive reports and pay up and look pleasant. But this major displayed a most unpleasant disregard for proper conventions.

"Now, look here, Finegan," said the major abruptly, "I'm not at all satisfied with the progress of your investigations and I intend to take a hand myself. I'm going to advertise in all the Melbourne daily papers for the information that I want."

Mr. Finegan's jaw dropped.

"This is what I intend to say," continued the major, who had hastily pencilled a few lines on the back of an envelope. "To boarding-house keepers and others. Fifty pounds reward. Any person who provided a Mrs. Robertson from India with board and lodging in Melbourne or suburbs in the year 188- will oblige by communicating with Messrs. Sharp and Stringer, Solicitors, Collins Street. All communications strictly confidential."

Mr. Finegan groaned. He could have kept the inquiry going for six months at least if he had been let alone. And now here was this bull-headed client taking the whole thing out of his hands with a horrible practicality that threatened to produce definite results forthwith.

"I'll have that inserted in the newspapers at once, Finegan," continued the major, "and we'll see what will happen. Go round now and Mrs. Burke will give you something to eat. You may as well stay here for a few days until I see what turns up in answer to the advertisement. I'll make you bookkeeper at the store to stop people from talking."

The major inserted his advertisement in the Melbourne dailies and also in the weeklies, and several people received sharp shocks when their eyes fell on it.

Laura Martin in Melbourne turned white when she saw the advertisement. Fifty pounds would be acceptable enough, of course, but how did she know what use the solicitors intended to make of the information when they got it? She had a wholesome dread of the law courts, having once been a witness in a case between a dressmaker and a lady customer who refused to accept an ill-fitting garment. The badgering that Mrs. Martin got from the dressmaker's counsel on that occasion made an abiding impression upon her. There was nothing that she would not cheerfully endure rather than be cross-examined again by any legal practitioner.

Moreover, Mrs. Martin was very uneasy in her own mind over her share in the double adoption of Mrs. Robertson's twin babies. It was possible that the adoption of the first baby by Mrs. Hesseltine had some connection with Mrs. Robertson's mysterious disappearance, and as for the second baby, Humphry, whom she had brought up herself, it was very undesirable that the circumstances under which he vanished from Melbourne should be investigated by any solicitors.

On the whole, Mrs. Martin decided to hold her tongue and do without the fifty pounds reward.

Mrs. Hesseltine, too, experienced a severe twinge of conscience when her eye fell on the advertisement, as she was turning over the pages of her weekly paper. Why on earth should a firm of Melbourne solicitors be hunting up Mrs. Robertson, the lady who had so mysteriously vanished after handing over one of her twin babies for adoption by the mistress of Mindaroona? It must be the same lady. It was most unlikely that there could be two Mrs. Robertsons from India staying in a Melbourne boarding-house twenty years ago. Probably some relative of Mrs. Robertson had instructed the solicitors to get the information, and in that case they would of course discover that Mrs. Robertson had given birth to twin sons before she disappeared.

What position would Mrs. Hesseltine occupy in that case with regard to Harold? Could the relatives take Harold away from her in spite of the agreement signed by the mother? And how could she herself face Harold if he learnt from strangers that he was not her son? Moreover, what would the major say about it? She had thought that she was practising a piece of innocent and harmless duplicity in bringing up Harold as her own son, for Simon Hesseltine had grimly accepted the situation right up to his death, and Mrs. Martin, who was the only other person who knew the true facts, had the best reasons for keeping silence.

Grace Hesseltine fell to wondering who was the unknown relative of Mrs. Robertson, and what was his object—she felt sure it was a man—in attempting to disinter the past. Already she began to hate and fear the unknown investigator.

There was one other person at Mindaroona who saw the advertisement and read it with positive dismay. This was Harold, who up to the Shaleville visit had supposed himself to be Harold Hesseltine, and who had ever since carried about with him the burden of a secret which made it difficult for him to accept his adopted mother's affection without revealing his knowledge of her duplicity.

When Harold read the advertisement he turned faint and sick with sudden apprehensions. Who could the stranger be who was endeavouring to trace the movements of 'Mrs. Robertson from India' in Melbourne twenty years earlier?

He left the house quickly and jumped on his own special hack that was tied up to the fence outside. "Tell my mother I won't be back till late, Mick," he called to the rouseabout, and, touching old Hailstorm with the spur, dashed away on a ten-mile ride to the station boundary.

He had plenty of time to think as he cantered over the springy turf, while old Hailstorm reefed and snatched at the bit in the pure joy of life and movement.

"My adoptive mother must never find out who the new boundary-rider is," he muttered to himself, "or there'll be the deuce to pay." And then he lost himself in thought.

Surely it was impossible, incredible that the woman who had been as a mother to him from his infancy could have any secret knowledge of his real mother—or could be even remotely connected with her disappearance. He felt himself growing cold all over at the bare thought of it.

Yet Humphry, his brother, was full of dark suspicions, and had come to Mindaroona to watch.

Old Hailstorm threw the distance lightly behind him that morning, and presently the boundary fence dividing Mindaroona from the Linton's place, Yarralla, came into view. It was a well-known track for the grey, because it led to a favourite meeting-place of Harold and Leonie, just over the crest of the hill, from the summit of which they could see the sea in the distance and the long trails of smoke from the passing steamers.

The boundary-rider's hut stood under a clump of blue gums in the corner of the Mindaroona paddock, and a man in shirtsleeves, breeches, rough leggings, and spurs was straining a new top wire in the dividing fence with a wire-strainer.

"Hullo," said Harold, "you're acting the part all right, I see. Come and sit down on this log, for I've something important to tell you." He tied old Hailstorm to the fence, and, sitting on the log, pulled a newspaper out of his pocket and showed Humphry the startling advertisement that he had seen in it.

Humphry read the advertisement through carefully. "Somebody else is on the search too!" he ejaculated. "Wonder who it can be."

"I've been trying to guess," said Harold, "and I'll admit I'm beaten. It can't be either of our adoptive mothers, and they're the only people so far as we know who had any interest in—our mother."

"Well, it seems to me," said Humphry, scrutinising the advertisement again, "that the advertiser who is behind Sharp and Stringer is hardly likely to get any response to his request, or perhaps I should say to her request, for it may be a woman. Mrs. Martin will hold her tongue on my account, and Mrs. Hesseltine is hardly likely to assist in uncovering a mystery in which she is evidently involved herself."

Harold drew figures in the dust with the point of his riding-switch. "I hope that you'll be able to find some clue soon, old man," he said, laying his hand affectionately on Humphry's shoulder. "Every day that you are here increases the risk that my moth—that Mrs. Hesseltine may find you out, and also that Finegan's discovery of you may bring the police out to take you back to Victoria in spite of your innocence. I shall never be able to rest now until this dreadful mystery is cleared up. I feel that I have not the right to look Leonie in the face and offer her my love, for I am not Harold

60

Hesseltine of Mindaroona, but nameless, a nobody's child, the son of a mother who gave me up and of a father who never saw me. Oh, it is terrible, terrible!"

Humphry, too, was deeply moved. He stood up and cast his eyes round the magnificent well-grassed Mindaroona paddocks with something like despair. And then his gaze fell on the blue Pacific in the distance and on the smoke of a passing steamer far out on the horizon. "It's a big search," he answered, "but I'm bound to go through with it. If Mrs. Hesseltine can't throw any light on the riddle we must try another way. But I have a feeling that somewhere within range of my eyes even here I shall find the traces that I am looking for." Again his gaze travelled all round the horizon, searching the rolling country to north and west and south—and to east the blue segment of the ocean, above which the last trail of smoke from a disappearing steamer still lingered.

"What are you going to do about—Mrs. Hesseltine?" asked Harold, boggling at the unfamiliar style of speaking about the woman who had taught him to regard her as his mother.

"That'll be your job," said Humphry with determination. "I cannot go near her. But you must see her and speak to her this very day. You must find out what she knows about our real mother. If she knows anything at all, I'll find a way to make her speak—you may trust me for that." Humphry's dark eyes sparkled. It was plain that he would consider neither man nor woman in the prosecution of the great quest.

But when Harold mounted old Hailstorm for the return journey his heart was as heavy as lead. He dreaded the coming interview with the woman who had played upon him this enormous and unheard-of trick, who had pretended to him that he was the son of her body when in fact he was the son of an unknown, strange woman who had drifted mysteriously into Australia, and had drifted as mysteriously away from it again. Why had the mistress of Mindaroona done this thing? She might be able to tell him something more of the mother who had given him up and of the father who was said to have died so long ago in a far country. But would she?

61

"Coo-ee," a fresh young voice sounded across the paddock, and, looking up, Harold saw Leonie and Marion Bingham cantering across the turf towards the boundary fence.

"Quick! Into the hut, Humphry!" he shouted, and Humphry disappeared just as the two girls reached the slip panel.

"Who is it you were talking to, Harold?" called Leonie, reining up at the other side of the fence.

"Only the new boundary-rider," replied Harold, and then, dismounting, he put down the slip panel and let the girls come through. "Come along, Leonie. Come along, Miss Bingham. I'll give you a race." And away he went at a smart gallop, eager to draw off the girls from the dangerous locality of the new boundary-rider's hut.

Leonie and Marion followed him, but not before Humphry, peering through the little square window of the hut, had seen them, recognising Leonie again in a moment and wondering who her companion could be—that beautiful, graceful girl who turned her head to scan the hut as she rode away, swaying to the long gallop of her horse like a reed that moves in a summer wind.

She had passed him by without seeing him. But he had seen her. And he made up his mind at once to see her again.

CHAPTER VII

THE ARRIVAL OF GULAB SINGH

The longer Finegan thought over the extra-ordinary resemblance between the young iron-worker at Shaleville, whom he positively identified as Humphry Robertson, and the young squatter of Mindaroona, who was well known to everybody in the neighbourhood as Mr. Harold Hesseltine, the more convinced he became that here was a secret which it would pay him to unravel.

After that terrible experience on the top of the blast furnace Finegan could not bring himself to denounce Humphry as the man who was wanted for the bank embezzlement in Victoria. Besides, he argued, there was surely a mistake somewhere. It was impossible that a thief would leap into the anteroom of hell to save the man who was about to arrest him.

But there was clearly some close connection between Harold Hesseltine and Humphry Robertson, alias Scott. Tim Finegan felt himself trembling on the verge of a great discovery. He had ascertained that Humphry left the ironworks on the morning after the terrible experience in the ore-holder and had not since been seen by any one in Shaleville. But Harold Hesseltine was at Mindaroona.

Finegan decided to ride over from Caringal to Mindaroona. The major had gone out and nobody was about. It was a good opportunity to call round and have a chat with Mrs. Hesseltine's new cook. He had already made the acquaintance of Jeanie McPherson, and it would probably be easy to find out all that she knew about the young man whom he had seen with his own eyes deep in consultation with the ex-bank clerk from Melbourne who had endeavoured so unsuccessfully to sink his identity by securing a job in the great iron-works.

The major's new bookkeeper had some trouble in catching a

mount, but after a good deal of running about he succeeded in cornering a quiet old brown stock-horse and getting the saddle and bridle on him.

Cantering along the gently rising track to Mindaroona, wrapped in speculations as to the fate of the missing woman whose disappearance he was supposed to be investigating, he found his thoughts returning steadily to the puzzling similarity and secret connection between the young ironworker and the son and heir of Mindaroona.

But the whole thing was a tangle that was quite beyond his power to unravel.

He looked along the track that stretched away ahead of him and became aware of a curious figure toiling along on foot.

The old brown stock-horse, with his 'two-pence three-halfpence' canter, quickly over-hauled the pedestrian, and Finegan passed him without deigning a second glance, merely wondering to himself how the dickens so many Afghan hawkers managed to get into the country in spite of the Immigration Restriction Act.

The Afghan hawker sat on a stump to rest for a few minutes. As a matter of fact he was no more an Afghan than he was an Assyrian; though nine out of ten of his customers described him as being either one or the other, forgetting that the true Afghan is too good a soldier to be a successful pedlar and that the Assyrian Empire was finally blotted out about two thousand five hundred years ago.

This particular dark-skinned individual, who spat on the ground as Tim Finegan cantered past, throwing the dust into his face, happened to be a native of British India. What the temptation was that induced him to leave his native country, and by what mysterious devices he succeeded in making his way to Australia, are matters that rested between himself and the deities of his heathen mythology.

In all probability he followed out some course of action similar to that which is so successfully adopted by the ever-increasing horde of dark-skinned Asiatics who pop up in the remotest regions of the Bush with enigmatical grins upon their

64

visages and well-filled packs of cheap jewellery and feminine finery on their backs. No one knows whence they come or whither they go. The important fact is that they are there and that most of them are quite ready to bully and frighten white womenfolk if the men are away from the hut when the 'Assyrian' happens to come down like a wolf on the fold.

Gulab Singh—for that was his name according to the exemption certificate which procured him admission to the Commonwealth—on the ground that he was a former resident of Australia returning after a visit to his native country—picked up his pack once more and plodded on, heading for Mindaroona, where he hoped to dispose of a good portion of his stock. He had a special side-line in fortune-telling, which he found a particularly remunerative art in the Bush, especially among the womenkind. He trudged along hopefully in the wake of the dust-surrounded horseman.

When Tim Finegan reached the fence at the back of the homestead he dismounted and hung his bridle over a post, whistling hopefully, and quite regardless of the scowl on the face of Ah Tong, Mrs. Hesseltine's valued and highly paid horticulturist, who was watering his asparagus bed in the adjoining vegetable garden.

"Good-day to you, Jeanie," said Tim Finegan politely as he opened the gate and walked into the enclosure; "sure 'tis beautiful dryin' weather to-day." He looked with respectful admiration at the well-covered clothes-lines upon which Jeanie McPherson, Mrs. Hesseltine's new treasure, not long from Peebles per favour of the Immigration Bureau, was performing the last joyous rites of washing-day.

Jeanie McPherson paused in the act of pinning an article of feminine underwear of generous dimensions on the clothes-line, and hurriedly removing two wooden clothes-pegs from between her glistening little white teeth, turned her blushing face towards the new-comer.

"Hech, Mester Finegan, how ye frichtened me!" said the maiden; "but come richt in tae the hoose and hae a crack."

"You wantee catch welly ni lettucee, Jee Nee?" called Ah Tong, popping his forbidding countenance over the light paling fence that separated the vegetable garden from the kitchen premises, and brandishing the material for a succulent salad most invitingly. Ah Tong displayed an ingratiating smile that might be called seraphic, if seraphs wore pigtails and showed long yellow pointed teeth when they smiled.

"Nae, nae," cried pretty Jeanie with a deprecatory wave of her plump little hands, "I'm no wantin' onything at a' the noo." She ran to Tim Finegan as if for protection, and seemed to be quite relieved in her mind when she found herself beside him. "I'm sae frichtened o' the gairdiner," she explained in a stage whisper; "I dinna ken what I'm tryin to dae when he speirs aboot me vegetables."

Tim Finegan was always ready to console a poor girl in distress. He took one of Jeanie's shapely hands in his own and stroked the back of it with broad human sympathy. "Don't cry, my dear," he said kindly; "I'll take care that the blooming Chow keeps on his own side of the fence."

"Aim nae greetin'," sniffed Jeanie, as bravely as she could, "but a never saw a theng like that i' Peebles, an' I'm fair scairt, I'm tellin' ye, when it glowers at me."

The grinning mask of Ah Tong above the paling fence was distorted with rage when Finegan continued to stroke the hand that was imprisoned in his own, and even to add other little endearments which his experience suggested as proper to the situation, such as putting his arm around the jimp waist and chucking the agitated lassie under her dimpled chin.

Ah Tong disappeared, but jealous wrath was plainly stamped upon his ugly face, and he muttered incoherently to himself as he flung the rejected lettuce on the path and danced on it. "Me give 'im whaffor bimeby," he gabbled darkly, while Finegan improved the occasion in the romantic neighbourhood of the well-laden clothes-line.

"Tell me, Jeanie," pursued Tim Finegan encouragingly, "what sort of a young fellow is Mr. Harold, and how does he get on with his mother? That young chap has quite taken my fancy."

66

"Weel now, Mester Finegan, I'm thenkin' that somethin' is wrang wi' Mester Harold an' his young leddy ower by Yarralla. It gars me greet to see them the noo sae far apairt, an' weel I ken that somethin's come between the laddie an' the lassie."

"Ah!" said Finegan; "since when?"

"Sence Mester Harold stayed out i' Shaleville for hauf the nicht," said Jeanie in a whisper, her large blue eyes agoggle with puzzled disapproval. "Do ye think, Mester Finegan, that he found some ither lassie i' Shaleville?"

"Not he," said Finegan confidently.

"Weel noo, I'm tellin' ye," continued Jeanie, "his mither's hairdly spoken tae him since that nicht, an' Miss Leonie seems to keep oot o' his way, an' the major when he comes to see the mistress will be settin' glowerin' at his ain toes for minutes thegither sayin' naething at a', an' the mistress looks aften eneuch like as if she'd been speirin' for ghaisties, an' I'm no that comfortable that I thocht to be in Mindaroona."

Jeanie was on the verge of tears, and Tim Finegan, while consoling her to the best of his ability, reflected that certainly there was something wrong at Mindaroona.

Was it possible that the trouble could be connected with the disappearance of the woman who had vanished twenty years ago. That disappearance he knew was in part, at any rate, the cause of the major's preoccupation, but then the major had told him definitely that he had not confided the subject of the search to anybody. It was almost inconceivable that Mrs. Hesseltine, or Harold, or Leonie Linton could know anything about it.

Finegan had his own idea about the major's reason for investigating the disappearance of Mrs. Harrington. "Been making love to her in India, of course," he said to himself sagely, "an' afraid she'll turn up again an' queer his pitch with the widow." Well, as long as the major paid him he was quite willing to continue the search. At the same time he felt that the atmosphere of suspicion at Mindaroona, the rift between Harold on the one hand and his mother and fiancee on the other, and the sudden appearance at Shaleville of Humphry Robertson, the ex-bank clerk from

Melbourne, who was as like Harold as one new shilling is like another, were irritating and perplexing factors in the main problem. If he could only find out what the connection was between Humphry Robertson and Harold Hesseltine, and what scheme they were jointly pursuing, he felt that it would be a distinct step in advance.

"See here, Jeanie, my girl," said Tim Finegan suddenly, "have you ever heard since you came here that Mr. Harold had a brother?"

"A brither!" ejaculated Jeanie, in surprise. "Nae, nae, the laddie has nae brither at a'. There's just himsel'."

"How long has old Simon Hesseltine, his father, been dead?"

"A dinna richtly ken, but lang Tammas the stockman telt me that the auld man never cud bear to look at the bairn frae the day he first set his een on him. An' Mistress Hesseltine never had but the ane. Gude maircy, what is that?"

It was Gulab Singh, who had just arrived and was looking over the gate. With the calm assurance of his profession, he slipped back the bolt and entered with his pack, solemn-visaged, imperturbable, business-like.

"Missy want to buy anything to-day?" he remarked in astonishingly good English. "Very good ribbon, very good handkerchief, or some nice pearl earrings?"

But Jeanie sprang back in alarm from the fluent stranger. His dusky beauty did not appeal to her. Her trained eye saw at once that his turban called loudly for the washtub, and she also remarked that he wore his nails a good deal longer than was considered fashionable in Peebles.

"Dinna pit oot the fairings here," she cried, "but ye can bide a wee whiles I'm tellin' the mistress. Maybe she'll ca' for ye on the front verandah."

She was off like an arrow, and Finegan inly cursed the intruder, who had broken in upon a line of investigation that was not only agreeable but likely to produce results.

"Hello, King Billy," began Finegan glibly, "how long you bin hump Matilda in this pfeller country, eh?"

"I spik the English quite well," remarked the Indian person calmly. "I learned it first in Government school at Lahore. If you will so kindly make the conversation in English, I am very pleased to give you the informations."

"Gee-long!" exclaimed Finegan, surprised out of himself; "I suppose you'll be standing for Parliament next?"

"It is possible," observed Gulab Singh calmly. "At Government school of Lahore I perused the works of John Stuart Mill, Macaulay, Tennyson, Ruskin, and Matthew Arnold. I am supporter of principles of political liberty. I received much education at Lahore. I know the doctrines of free trade, also of protection. I consider that cumbrous and antiquated system of land tenure in India's great obstacle to development of country. All these matters I learnt, but found avenues of using knowledge much, oh! very much restricted, wherefore I became butler to officer sahib at rupees 10 per mensem. Subsequently I came to this country. Now I am business man. Oh yes, very good business man. Can I sell you something to-day, a pipe or very fine jewelled pin?"

"My oath, you're the one!" said Finegan. "By the way, haven't you got any land yet?"

"Not yet, but soon yes. I am applicant at ballot for many eligible blocks. Presently I shall secure one of those blocks. Many of my countrymen have them already in this State. In meanwhile I sell goods on commission—very good commission—and I also tell past and future events. Shall I tell you past and future events?"

"You might tell me a bit of your own past. Whose exemption certificate did you beg, borrow, or steal in India, eh? And how did you manage to bluff the Customs officer? Do you know that as a prohibited immigrant you're liable under the Act of 1901 to six months' imprisonment and then deportation?" Gulab Singh waved a deprecating palm. "You do not remember that I am educated. I know free trade and protection. I also know politics. Your Government will not send me to prison for six months because it would make much trouble. Questions would be asked in British Parliament, also in National Congress. How can a British subject be imprisoned for crime of being in a British dominion? Your law says that you can imprison me for six months, but if you do it bombs will be thrown in Dacca and there will be riots in Lahore. Already there is much trouble owing to treatment of my countrymen in the Transvaal. Your Government must not make more trouble here. The position is delicate. You see, I am educated. I study politics. Perhaps I shall be a member of the first Indian Parliament. Who knows? Meanwhile, here comes the female servant of the house. I am perhaps requested to display my merchandise. It is well."

"Mester Finegan, Mester Finegan!" cried Jeanie McPherson, waving shapely arms from afar, "wull ye please to stop yer havering and send the black mon roun' the hoose to the front verandy? The mistress an' the major wad be glad tae speak wi' him."

"Hold on a minute," said Finegan, who had been regarding the gifted stranger with ill-dissembled amazement. "What was the name of the place in India that you said you came from?"

"Tilgit," said Gulab Singh calmly, as he walked off with his pack towards the front verandah of the homestead.

CHAPTER VIII

YELLOW AGAINST BLACK

As Gulab Singh with his pack on his back turned the angle of the house and opened up the verandah upon which Major McLean and Mrs. Hesseltine were reclining in long cane chairs placed side by side, he gave a start of astonishment. Then, composing his features again into their customary Oriental impassivity, he proceeded to open his pack.

His goods were of excellent quality. Scent, ribbons, gloves, handkerchiefs, silk stockings, shoes, a few lace blouses, pipes, ties, braces, socks, and imitation Panama hats. Mrs. Hesseltine bought a few articles and so did the major.

Gulab Singh salaamed.

"Some of these fellows are great practitioners of the occult," whispered the major to Mrs. Hesseltine. "I have seen them do some extraordinary things in India. Suppose we ask him if he knows anything of the craft of yogi."

Mrs. Hesseltine assented, although she felt strangely nervous of the Indian with his dirty turban and his long nails.

"I say, what's your name and what part of India do you come from?" inquired the major, lighting another cigarette.

"I am Gulab Singh, sahib," replied the hawker, "from the Punjaub. I spik the English very well. I am educated at Government school of Lahore. I have perused the works of Mill, Ruskin, Tennyson, and Macaulay."

"The deuce you have! Do any yogi tricks?"

"I do not make tricks, sahib," said Gulab Singh, drawing himself up with dignity, "but by meditation and fasting I have power to reveal past and unfold future."

"By Jove! you're just the man I'm looking for," said the major, half in jest and half in earnest. "Put down your pack and let us see what you can do. You shan't lose by it, I promise you. Let's have a bit of the past—my past, of course—for a start."

Gulab Singh salaamed once more. "Your honour shall be obeyed," he said very solemnly.

The Indian left his pack on the edge of the verandah and stalked across the lawn to a patch of young gum saplings near the gate. He pulled a handful of the leaves; then he bent down and picked up a small quantity of stiff, clayey soil from Mrs. Hesseltine's rose-border.

Returning to the verandah, he squatted on his haunches in front of the major, moistened the clay with saliva, and stuck it upon a gum leaf, which he placed in the palm of his left hand. He rubbed the clay until the surface was smooth and shining. Then, muttering some incomprehensible jargon of words, he stared steadfastly into the polished clay.

Mrs. Hesseltine sat up in her chair nervously expectant. She could not take her eyes off that squatting sinister figure for an instant.

"Well, Gulab Singh," said the major with a forced laugh, "what can you see there?"

"I see nothing yet," said Gulab Singh. He polished the clay surface with his long black forefinger. There was an anxious pause. Again he murmured his mysterious jargon.

"I'm afraid you're a bit of a humbug," said the major lightly, but to Mrs. Hesseltine's ear there seemed to be a note of relief in his voice.

"The mirror is clouding over," said Gulab Singh in his low, monotonous voice. "Now it clears again. I see—a woman."

The major positively jumped and Mrs. Hesseltine looked at him in a scared kind of way. The tension was becoming quite painful.

"The woman is lying on a long chair on the verandah of a bungalow. There are mountains all around. They are high mountains with snow on them. The woman is very pale. Her eyes and hair are dark. She looks as though she had been weeping."

"Yes, yes!" said the major excitedly. "Go on, man, go on."

"I see an officer in uniform riding up to the gate. He dismounts. He approaches the bungalow. He speaks to the woman."

"What is he like, man, what is he like?"

"I—I cannot see his face, it is turned away. Ah, now he turns it towards me."

"Well, well, can you recognise the features? Who is it?"

"Sahib, it is you."

Mrs. Hesseltine stifled a scream and sat up on her chair, wide-eyed, staring at the Indian. The major's face was pale under its tan. This was certainly interesting.

"The sahib and the mem-sahib seem to be quarrelling," continued the Indian in his monotonous, passionless voice. "Now he comforts her and kisses her. She puts her hand to her breast, she sways to and fro, she faints. There is a plain gold ring on the third finger of her left hand."

The major looked with amazement at the preposterous figure squatting before him on the verandah.

"I see a child's face," said the Indian. "It is a shadowy face. It is looking over the shoulder of the fainting mem-sahib. I see it more plainly. Sahib, where is your son?"

"Here, I've had enough of this," said the major, whose face was pale and ghastly. "I have no son. I have never had a son. Get out of this, you offspring of Shaitan, and take your devil-tricks somewhere else."

He threw a couple of sovereigns into the extended palm, and went abruptly into the house to get a brandy and soda, for his tongue was sticking to the roof of his mouth.

Mrs. Hesseltine lay back in her long chair with closed eyes. The strangest thoughts were whirling through her brain. The major had been married when he was in India and had kept it a secret from her and from everybody else who knew him in Australia. This fakir said that the major's wife had had a son. Who was the wife and where was the son? Mrs. Hesseltine simply dared not allow herself to think any longer. She opened her eyes again and looked around. The Indian was just walking away with his pack.

And as he disappeared round the corner the garden gate opened and Harold entered. How changed that once lighthearted boy had become! She felt an unspoken accusation in his stare.

"I've brought Leonie and Marion home to tea, mother," said Harold quietly, and as he spoke the two girls, still in their riding-habits, came up and kissed Mrs. Hesseltine affectionately.

"We've had such a lovely ride," chattered Leonie, "haven't we, Marion? And Harold was really quite gay and like his old self, weren't you, Harold? We went through the home paddocks and across the creek and then over the Black Mountain to the boundary-rider's hut, and back by the old track to the dam, and so home. But we didn't see the new boundary-rider. I believe the poor man was shy. He disappeared into his hut like a lizard into a hole in a rock when he saw us coming. Didn't he, Marion?"

But Harold changed the subject and switched the conversation on to a new track with a jolt. "Rum-looking chap, that old Hindoo hawker," he remarked abruptly. "I hope he won't fall foul of Ah Tong. The gardener is getting more pernicketty every day, mother. You'll really have to get rid of him. He has got to talking to himself now."

"He gives us better cauliflowers than ever grew at Mindaroona before, dear," said Mrs. Hesseltine, "and as long as he does that he can talk to himself as much as he likes, if it amuses him."

"Oh, don't you know what's the matter with the poor fellow?" put in Leonie. "He's head over ears in love with that pretty Scotch lassie in the kitchen, but hard-hearted Jeanie won't have anything at all to do with him. She confided to me one day last week that he asked her to 'mally' him, and I gathered that her 'hoots' and 'toots' anent the proposal were anything but complimentary to him."

"Probably he's jealous," said Marion reflectively. "There's nothing makes an ordinary man so bad-tempered as jealousy—unless it's drink. And I suppose a Chinese feels the same way about it."

"But he hasn't anybody to be jealous of," said Mrs. Hesseltine with a smile. "Poor Jeanie hasn't seen an admirer since she has been

74

here, unless it's that mysterious man Finegan who has been staying up at Caringal, pretending to be the major's new bookkeeper."

"It's to be hoped Ah Tong won't get it into his head that he is being cut out by the gentleman from Ind—"

But the sentence was never finished. The three ladies on the verandah sprang to their feet as a long, unearthly, blood-chilling screech rose upon the air somewhere at the back of the homestead. They looked at each other open-eyed.

"Please stay here, mother," said Harold curtly, "and you too, Leonie and Marion. I'll go round and find out what's the matter. It sounded like Jeanie McPherson." He snatched up his heavy hunting-crop and rushed off to the back of the house, skirting the paling fence that divided the drying yard from the vegetable garden.

Harold was just in time to see Ah Tong scrambling over the six-foot paling fence with blood in his eye and a long-handled garden hoe in his hand. As the Chinaman was preparing to drop from the top of the fence, he caught his foot in the handle of the hoe and fell headlong into Jeanie's rubbish-bin, a large galvanised-iron receptacle full of potato peelings, eggshells, tea-leaves, and kitchen fat.

Harold could see at once that Gulab Singh was the objective of the attack. Finegan had ridden back to Caringal while the hawker was at the front of the house, and when Gulab Singh, chuckling quietly to himself, reappeared in the yard, he had a capital opportunity to make himself pleasant to the apple-cheeked damsel frae Peebles. Ah Tong, peering over the fence, had witnessed the colloquy. Here was a tragedy of jealousy in the true Elizabethan manner. The Chinaman was stung to madness by seeing Jeanie with her Othello, and it was the menace of his murderous demonstrations with the hoe that evoked that eldritch screech from Jeanie when she saw him actually scrambling over the fence.

As Harold ran forward with his hunting-crop raised, Ah Tong picked himself out of the rubbish bin and came on to the attack, a horrid spectacle.

"Get back, get back, you lunatic!" yelled Harold, making a wild swipe at the Chinaman with his hunting-crop.

Ah Tong darted back out of reach, and whirling the long-handled hoe with both hands, dealt the luckless youth a terrific crack on the head at long range and felled him to the ground.

Jeanie had fled to the furthest part of the yard, where she wedged herself into the corner, emitting short shrill shrieks in swift succession, but Gulab Singh stood his ground firmly with his back to one of the stout posts supporting the clothes-line in the middle of the yard. With all his shiftiness he came of a fighting race, and, moreover, he was not caught unprepared. From some mysterious recess of his frowsy garments he produced a long, wicked-looking knife, and as he gripped the horn handle with determination it was plain that the Chinaman would not have it all his own way.

Ah Tong, spurred to frenzy by his easy victory over Harold, surrendered himself to the fierce joy of running amok.

Uttering a tremendous yell, he rushed at the Indian, wielding the hoe in both hands, and whirling it round his head, let fly a terrific blow which would have smashed Gulab Singh's skull like an eggshell if it had taken effect.

But Gulab Singh ducked in the nick of time, and the Chinaman, missing his mark, overbalanced himself and staggered for a few yards as though about to fall. Before he could recover his stability the Indian was at him, and a slash of the long knife ripped open the Chinaman's sleeve and drew blood from a glancing cut.

Dropping the hoe, Ah Tong made a grab for the knife, which slipped from the Indian's grasp and fell to the ground. Seeing that his opponent was weaponless, the Chinaman wreathed his long gorilla-like arms around Gulab Singh and strove to throw him, but the Indian, though inferior in height and weight, was an accomplished wrestler and Ah Tong was speedily in difficulties. As they came to the ground the Chinaman was underneath, and the crash with which his head hit the stones would have taken all the fight out of most people.

But Ah Tong was sustained by the strength of temporary insanity. He gripped his opponent by the throat, and round and

76

round they rolled together, grunting, squeaking, and hissing as each sought to choke the life out of the other, or, as an alternative, to get possession of the long-bladed knife that still lay where it had been dropped.

The Chinaman was a distressful sight. He was covered with blood and tea-leaves and kitchen fat from the rubbish bin. His clothes were torn to shreds, and Gulab Singh had secured a good hold of his pigtail with one hand and of his throat with the other, so that he could vary his method of attack by alternately throttling his antagonist and banging his head on the ground.

But Ah Tong was still able to squeeze the Indian so hard in his iron grip that Gulab Singh could feel his ribs cracking, and it was difficult to say how the issue would have gone if the men had been left to fight it out without interference.

A diversion was soon at hand, however, for Jeanie began to scream with renewed vigour as the black man and the yellow man, locked in deadly mutual grips, began to roll nearer and nearer to the corner where she had taken refuge.

Mindaroona homestead was solidly built of stone, and the major was in the front of the house, but the voice of the Scotch lassie raised in frantic appeal for assistance reached him, and, leaping through the open French window, he made his way to the scene of action.

One glance at the maddened antagonists, who were rolling round and round, scratching, kicking, biting, squeezing, butting, punching, and throttling each other, covered in blood, and mud, and tea-leaves, and kitchen fat, was enough to show the major that it was a case for drastic treatment, and that at the same time a third party interfering would stand a good chance of being murdered.

Compared with the contest between the Indian native and the Chinese, an ordinary dog-fight would have been a mere unexciting tiff.

As they rolled and scuffled on the ground under the clothes-line, Ah Tong had grabbed at a waving streamer of finely laundered linen with disastrous results. In its fall it brought down other items of the weekly wash, and when the major arrived on the scene the grimy combatants were impeded in their efforts to assassinate each other by being tangled up with delicate habiliments, frilled, billowy, and lacy, of every size and shape.

Jeanie McPherson in her corner wrung her hands despairingly over the ruined garments, ravished from their protecting clothes-line and dragged in the mire.

The major was not lacking in physical courage, but he was faddy on the subject of physical cleanliness, and he shrank from personal contact with two animated rubbish-bins. However, he was also a man of resource, quick to devise a plan and prompt to execute it.

Running to the tool-house, he dragged out a length of stout garden hose, and hastily screwed the brass-fitted end of it to the standard at the side of the yard. Minderoona was noted for its splendid water supply.

Grasping the business end of the hose, which terminated in a long brass nozzle, the major called to Jeanie to turn on the tap. There was an excellent pressure, as it happened, and the powerful jet of water that leaped from the nozzle as the major carefully aimed it took all the fight out of Ah Tong and loosened the tenacious grip of Gulab Singh effectively.

No human beings could withstand such a deluge, and the half-drowned combatants staggered to their feet, seeking escape at all costs. The major kept the hose on Ah Tong until the dripping Chinaman fairly ran from the yard and disappeared into the adjoining paddock. And that was the last of Ah Tong that Mindaroona ever saw.

Then the major turned his attention to Gulab Singh, who seemed to be in a bad way, and also to Harold Hesseltine, who was sitting up on the ground holding his head in both hands. Harold was a bit dazed, and there was a lump as big as an egg on the side of his head, but the major gave a sigh of relief when he saw that the boy was not seriously injured.

Presently, as the major bent over the Indian, gazing intently into his face, Gulab Singh opened his eyes. The douching that he had got from the garden hose had washed off all the dust with which his face was encrusted and his features obscured when he first arrived. It had also washed off the blood from the late encounter.

He looked up at the major and his lips curled in a faint grin. "It is a pity that you came, sahib, a great pity. I would have killed that pig-tailed child of Shaitan with my two hands."

But the major was staring at the hawker with incredulity and amazement stamped on every feature. "I know your face," he said at last; "your name is not Gulab Singh. You are the man who was my servant at Tilgit. You are Muhammad Bahksh."

And then the significance of the incident struck him, and his brain reeled.

So this was the explanation of the amazing bit of jugglery that had been worked off on him by the Indian. Muhammad Bahksh had recognised him at once, and had drawn upon memory, not upon second-sight, for that astonishing description of the scene on the verandah of the bungalow in Tilgit. He had remembered the major's wife perfectly. But why, then, had he talked about the major's son?

The major lifted the man up and placed him in a sitting posture with his back against the heavy square post supporting the clothes-lines. Placing both hands upon the Indian's shoulders, he stared him straight between the eyes.

"Now, Muhammad Bahksh," he said, "tell me the truth. What did you mean when you asked me about my son?"

"Sahib," said the man, drawing his breath with difficulty, "it is true that I am Muhammad Bahksh. Yet, having bought from Gulab Singh the paper which allowed the possessor to pass freely into this country, I became Gulab Singh. It is nothing. What matters one name or another?"

"But why did you speak a little while ago about my son?" persisted the major; "for I have no son, nor have I seen my wife since I returned from fighting against the Zakka Khels."

"Sahib," muttered the Indian, "a blind mule sees nothing, but one that hath two good eyes can see the grass growing. Were you not married to the mem-sahib for nearly three months before she went away?"

The major nodded excitedly.

"And do you not remember the day when she fainted on the verandah of the bungalow?"

Again the major motioned assent.

"Sahib, the ayah Shaibalini told me then that the mem-sahib would be the mother of a child. For the mem-sahib had told her. And that is why I asked you just now, saying, 'Where is your son?' for assuredly it is a son, and he still lives."

The major started up abruptly. "Come along into the house, Harold," he called to the young fellow, who was ruefully feeling the bump on his head, while Jeanie hovered round him, tearfully murmuring incomprehensible regrets. "Come into the house and get your head bathed."

He threw a glance at the Indian before he left. "I'll be back to speak further with you, Muhammad Bahksh, on this matter," he called to the adventurous hawker. "There are things that I have yet to learn concerning you."

But as soon as the major had entered the house Muhammad Bahksh, alias Gulab Singh, rose to his feet and picked up his pack. He had no desire to be questioned further concerning the transaction with Gulab Singh. It seemed to the student of Mill and Macaulay quite possible that the troopers whom he occasionally met in the Bush might subject him to humiliating restraints on his personal liberty if they ascertained from the major that he was Muhammad Bahksh and not Gulab Singh at all.

Accordingly, the Indian drifted out from Mindaroona as he had drifted in, and when the major returned after bathing Harold's head there was no sign of the wanderer who had conveyed to him the startling intelligence that he was a father.

He the father of a child! It was quite likely, although he had never thought of it before. Here, then, was a link with the past which made it impossible for him to cut those old days in India out of his life as he thought he could have done.

If the Indian was right and a son had been born to him, that son would be twenty years of age. The major felt a strange thrill in his heart.

He had a twofold reason now for tracing the movements of his wife, and he determined to apply himself to the task with redoubled energy.

CHAPTER IX

A CLUE AND A KANGAROO HUNT

Old Simon Hesseltine had one good point, at any rate, for which he deserved to be kept in remembrance. He bred some good horses.

The Mindaroona brand was well known on every show-ground within a hundred miles of the station, and Wallaroo, the big, strapping chestnut that Humphry mounted a couple of mornings after his arrival, had more than once gained a place in the heavyweight hunters' competitions.

He was a big-boned horse, decidedly on the plain side, with a head like a portmanteau, and he stood nearly seventeen hands high, but in spite of his looks he could both jump and gallop, and he could stay for a week.

"Shure ye can ride him to hell an' back in the wan day," said Mike, the rouseabout, as he handed the horse over to Harold on the previous morning, "an' he'll niver lay a toe on anny fince all the way." So Harold handed him over to Humphry, and Humphry climbed into the saddle, purposing to ride out to the Black Mountain and interview Angus McPhee, the old shepherd who was with Simon Hesseltine before his marriage, and would doubtless remember Mrs. Hesseltine's return from Melbourne with the unexpected infant.

It would be strange, indeed, if Angus McPhee could not say definitely whether or not a strange lady had arrived from Melbourne soon after Mrs. Hesseltine's eventful holiday of twenty years earlier, and, if she did arrive then, how long she stayed and where she went on her departure.

Humphry felt certain that with the information to be derived from the old shepherd he would be able to clear up the first point about which he was in doubt, namely, whether his mother ever saw

Mrs. Hesseltine again after Mrs. Hesseltine left 'The Cedars' at St. Kilda. He had not told Harold of his intention to sound the old shepherd, because Harold was plainly disinclined to take any step likely to suggest that his adoptive mother had any sinister knowledge of his real mother's disappearance. Harold plainly shrank from facing the possibilities. He was not made of the same stern stuff as Humphry, much as he resembled him physically.

Humphry touched Wallaroo with the spur and the chestnut bounded forward, fighting for his head. When the old horse saw the fence at the end of the paddock he distinctly pricked his ears and gathered himself together. He sailed over it without a rap and Humphry surrendered himself to the pure joy of the rapid motion. For such a big, ungainly-looking horse Wallaroo had a wonderfully smooth canter, and the turf was green and springy after the winter rains.

With a good horse under him and the open country before him, no rider can carry black Care behind him for very long in Australia, in spite of the ancient poet, and Humphry speedily shook off all traces of gloom.

Wallaroo was a great natural jumper and he had also had plenty of practice. Moreover, he had always been ridden by a straight-goer, and consequently he did not know what it was to refuse. Humphry took a line as the crow flies from the boundary fence of Mindaroona, through the intervening Yarralla paddocks, back again into Mindaroona, and then across the creek into the scrub country fringing the Black Mountain.

Nothing stopped the chestnut. No fence was too stiff and no take-off too tricky for him, and when he got to the creek, which was forty feet across, with steep clay banks on both sides, he slid dexterously down the descent with his hind legs well under him and climbed the other side with a succession of bounds that made Humphry's teeth rattle.

Humphry had received explicit directions from Harold, and he soon made out the shepherd's hut. He also made out the shepherd himself sitting on a log, with a wall-eyed collie, which was watching the billy on the fire, and was quite ready to notify Mr. McPhee the moment that the water began to boil.

McPhee was over seventy and his sight was not too good, but the collie recognised an old acquaintance in Wallaroo and gave a couple of short, sharp barks, waving her tail in polite salutation. However, when Humphry threw his leg over the saddle and slid to the ground she growled, sniffing suspiciously.

"Wha's wrang wi' ye, Jess, ye auld fule?" said Angus McPhee, pausing for a moment in the operation of cutting up a pipeful. "A' never knew ye tae growl at Mesther Harold until the noo."

So that was it. The old man naturally took him for his brother. Well, perhaps it was just as well not to undeceive him.

"I just rode across, McPhee," said Humphry, "to tell you to leave a couple of killing sheep for the new boundary-rider."

"Oo aye, Mesther Harold."

"Foxes pretty bad lately?

"Oo aye, oo."

"How are the rabbits?"

"Fine."

Clearly this line of inquiry was not likely to lead to much. It might be advisable to alter the plan of attack.

"Will you have a drink, McPhee?"

"Drink o' what?"

"A drink of whisky. I've got my flask with me."

"Whaur is it?"

Humphry produced the flask and Angus McPhee's granite visage slowly assumed a human expression. But in all the years that he had known Harold Hesseltine he had never seen him produce whisky before. It was a strange and stirring event in the life of the shepherd. It was a new experience.

McPhee applied the flask to his lips and filled his mouth, which contained about half a tumblerful, with the neat spirit. He swallowed it slowly and then, reaching for his pannikin, drank about two teaspoonfuls of water.

"Ma respects tae ye, Mesther Harold," said the old man, whose tongue had been thawed from its frozen stiffness by the liquor. "I'm richt gled tae see ye. Gang oot o' this, ye auld fule, Jess, and don't be smellin' Mesther Harold's legs. I dinna ken what ye are thenkin' aboot."

At that point two big kangaroo-dogs, a brindled and a black, emerged from the bush, and the collie, with a final sniff of distrust at Humphry, went off to join them, remarking with eye, ear, mouth, and tail, as plainly as a dog could, that the visitor was not the person that he appeared to be, and that Angus McPhee was a dunderheaded old fool who could not see what was as plain as the nose on his face.

"Have another drink, McPhee?"

Again the solemn ritual was gone through, and Mr. McPhee's tongue received a second and even more generous dose of the useful lubricant.

"By the way, can you remember, McPhee, the time when you first saw Har—when you first saw me?"

"Oo aye, Mesther Harold. A mind weel when yer mither brocht ye hame wi' her frae Melbourne, whaur ye were born."

Ah! So Simon Hesseltine had told nobody, and not a soul on the station guessed what only he and his wife knew that the infant who was brought from Melbourne was no child of theirs but a stranger's baby. This was something, at any rate. If Angus McPhee, who knew most of Simon Hesseltine's secrets, had never learnt this one, it was certain that nobody else in the neighbourhood would be aware of it.

Humphry found himself marvelling at the secretiveness of Mrs. Hesseltine. After bluffing the whole neighbourhood into the belief that the baby was her own, she had never had the moral courage to acknowledge the deception when the child grew up. Her husband had died without disclosing the fact, and Mrs. Martin, far away at St. Kilda, was the only other person who knew that Mrs. Hesseltine's heir was not her son.

"Look here, McPhee, do you remember any lady coming to Mindaroona to see—my mother—soon after she brought—me— back with her from Melbourne?"

"Oo aye. There was a plenty leddies comin' to Mindaroona lang syne."

"Can you remember any of them?"

"Aye, aye. I mind them weel. Weel-looking leddies eneuch, but not like auld Simon's wife—nae, nae. She was the bonniest o' them a'."

"Would you know any of them if you saw them again?"

"Wad I ken the leddies I saw lang syne? Oo aye."

"Have you ever seen this lady before?" Humphry took the photograph of his mother from his inner breast-pocket and placed it before the astonished old shepherd.

Mr. Angus McPhee took the photograph into his own hands, and it would be understating the fact to say that he examined it carefully. He looked at it first with one eye closed and then with the other. He scrutinised it at arm's-length, and he peered into it at three inches from his face. He criticised it right side up and upside down. He even turned it over and examined the photographer's name on the back.

Humphry watched him with painful intentness. "Well, McPhee, have you ever seen that lady or not?"

"A winna gae sae far as tae say that A hae seen the bonnie leddy—an' A canna say for a fact that A hae not seen her," remarked Mr. McPhee cautiously. "Its verra posseeble, ye ken, that A hae seen her, an then again it's mair than likely that A hae not. But A can say this much—that A dinna remember to hae seen the leddy at Mindaroona, and sence she is such a bonnie leddy hersel' A thenk A shud hae remembered her. At ony rate it's mair than posseeble."

Humphry stamped his heel into the ground with chagrin. Was it for this that he had come so far? The evidence, however—if it could be called evidence—was negative as far as it went. Old McPhee did not remember to have seen the lady, and it was hardly likely that he would have forgotten her if he had seen her. It would be unsafe to take it for granted that Mrs. Robertson, as she had called herself, never arrived at Mindaroona, but if she did arrive there she must have come secretly and left hurriedly. She might easily have arrived without Angus McPhee being made aware of the fact, and as for her departure—Humphry would not allow himself to formulate his suspicions except so far as to suggest that it might have been very much to the interest of some third party that Mrs. Robertson's departure from Mindaroona should be unseen by any person.

"Wull ye tak the dogs wi' ye same as usual, goin' back, Mesther Harold? Likely ye'll see a kangaroo or two when ye're ridin' through the Bush."

The old man's voice broke in upon Humphry's ruminations and caused him to look up. He was not much in the mood for kangarooing, but it was necessary to keep up the deception.

If Harold usually took the dogs, he would take them too.

"All right, McPhee; better whistle them up."

The shepherd gave a long whistle and the two big kangaroo-dogs, with the collie close in their wake, came tearing out of a patch of timber and raced up to McPhee.

"The wind is easterly to-day, isn't it, McPhee?" said Humphry, letting his gaze go eastwards to the blue glitter of the ocean where the smoke from a couple of coasters could be seen far out on the horizon.

"Ay, ay," said the shepherd. "Ye can see the waves breakin' abune the Walrus Rock frae the top o' the hill. Yer auld father wad say tae me mony a time, 'Angus,' he wad say, 'the Government shud pit a bit licht-hoose on the cliff or there'll be a wrack oot there some black nicht, for the Walrus Rock is terrible dangerous in an easterly gale.'"

"Is it?"

"Ay indeed! It's richt across the mouth o' Blackfish Bay, ye ken. When I cam here lang syne Blackfish Bay was the port for Mindaroona an' had a wee bit jetty of its ain. Ye can see wha's left of it at low tide still. But there was ony a puir trade for the boats, an' they gied up callin' and the jetty sune fell tae pieces."

The old man maundered on, but Humphry's thoughts were far away.

"We'll hae the equeenoctial gales next month, forbye,"

continued McPhee, "an' when they comes they amaist blaws ma wee bit hoose inside oot. But ye'll be gangin' yer ways the noo, an' Tinker an' Sailor 'll gae wi' ye, for I seen scrub wallaby dune by the creek a week syne an' mayhap ye'll pit up a 'roo as well."

Humphry swung himself into the big stock-saddle with its great knee-pads, and Wallaroo moved off at a walk, followed by Sailor and Tinker, the brindled and black kangaroo-dogs. As the rider gathered up the bridle the horse broke into his long easy canter across the open ground, but Humphry pulled him into a walk again as they entered the belt of light timber on the lower slope of Black Mountain.

Sailor and Tinker were cruising in front. Half greyhound and half deerhound, they were the true breed for kangarooing, and, hunting altogether by sight and not by scent, they developed extraordinary keenness of vision as well as speed and activity in closely timbered country.

Humphry was sitting loosely in the saddle brooding, with the habit which had become a second nature with him, upon the chances of ever finding out what had happened to his mother and who his father was, when the big chestnut gave a bound that shifted the rider on to his neck and started forward at breakneck speed through the timber.

As Humphry clambered back into the saddle he realised that the horse had jumped a huge log and with his ears cocked was galloping in the wake of two flying forms, one brindled and one black, nearly a hundred yards in front. Humphry could not see the quarry, but he guessed that Sailor and Tinker had sighted a 'roo, and judging by the pace that they were making, they would soon be on top of him.

Clenching his teeth and taking a good grip with his knees, Humphry gave old Wallaroo his head, and that experienced animal took full charge of the hunt.

Away in front the black and brindled dogs seemed at times to be flying, as they leaped fallen trees and rose over patches of light scrub fully six feet high.

The big chestnut was wonderfully active, dodging the timber

88

without any apparent lessening of pace, turning and twisting like a hare, and judging his distances marvellously. Now and then he would buck over a log that the rider did not even see and squeeze between two trees where it seemed hopeless to make a passage.

Once Humphry ducked just in time to escape a branch that would certainly have split his skull if it had collided with it, and several times the big knee-pads saved his legs from blows that would have crippled him.

After a mile of this desperate stern-chasing in the timber the hunt emerged into open country, and at last Humphry saw the great grey shape of a regular 'old man' 'roo just in front of the dogs. They had skilfully headed the creature away from cover and now had it at their mercy in an open paddock.

Wallaroo was going great guns and pulling like a steam-engine. Humphry had forgotten all his troubles, and was thoroughly absorbed in the primitive excitement of the hunt.

A big post-and-rail fence bounded the paddock next to the thick timber, and Humphry saw the 'roo fly it only a few yards in front of the dogs. But the creature was almost done. It had travelled over two miles at a fast pace, and it evidently realised that it must be overhauled in a few strides more. Suddenly it halted, with its back against a solitary ring-barked gum, and sat up to make its last fight.

Tinker, the black dog, attacking in front, made a leap for the throat, but missed his grip, and fell back howling with a long red wound from the murderous hind foot that ripped him from neck to flank.

But the brindled dog was an older hand at the game. He hurled himself at the kangaroo, taking the creature sideways, and toppled him over. Next instant he had him by the throat, and the silver-grey vest was stained with scarlet.

It was at that moment that the big chestnut approached the four-railer, going like a railway train, but neither horse nor man saw the top wire stretched a foot above the highest rail.

Both the kangaroo and the dogs had jumped it clean.

Humphry gave the chestnut his head and took a good grip with his knees. The horse was going at racing pace.

Ping!

That was the last sound that Humphry heard as the chestnut turned over.

* * * * *

How pleasant it was to be paddling with his little bucket and spade on the St. Kilda beach near Hegarty's baths. He would certainly take that big jelly-fish home in his bucket and show it to mother.

There! He was glad to be in knicker-bockers at last, instead of being dressed like a little girl, and Tommy Parsons next door was a jolly nice friend. His games of pirates, bushrangers, and Indians were just the thing. If he could only have a sword and a pistol! He would ask mother to get them for him next time she went into Collins Street by the old bus that went along the dusty St. Kilda road.

Speech-day at the Melbourne Grammar School. And he had got two prizes. But, better still, he had got into the second for his bowling and had made twenty-three against Wesley second, besides getting five wickets for thirty-two. Wouldn't mother be pleased about his prizes!

But where was his mother? He had lost her. He was looking for her everywhere. How could a person have two mothers? And why was that policeman asking for him at the door?

Something wrong at the bank. Why did his mother think it best for him to go away? He had done nothing wrong. What! She wasn't his mother at all. She had only adopted him. His real mother had disappeared, and nobody knew what had happened to her. Well, he would find her somehow.

Surely she could not be there, on top of the blast furnace, where it was snowing. How terrifying those coloured flames were as they leaped up flickering and twisting into the black night. And how strange the falling snowflakes looked when the light fell on them.

90

Snowflakes falling, falling, falling. Red flames rising, rising, rising.

Ha! He must get out of this terrible place. He was sliding, sliding, sliding into a sea of fire. But he must never let go his grip of that man's collar—never, even if his companion dragged him down into the molten hell.

God! The very ground that he lay on was sinking—into the furnace. The pillar of fire already scorched his hair—and blinded him. He could see no more. But still he must grip the collar of the inanimate thing beside him.

Was that his guardian angel—that mysterious figure—gigantic, cloaked, and helmeted? No. It was Sergeant Box, and they were saved! Life opened before him again—life and time instead of death and eternity. Life to continue the search and time to find the woman whom he sought.

Where should he seek her first? On the lands of that other woman who had taken away her son. He would carry the pursuit to the very ends of the earth.

How well the chestnut galloped! How actively he turned and twisted and how brilliantly he jumped! Only one more fence.

Ping!

* * * * *

"Are you better now?"

Humphry opened his eyes and found himself looking into the pale and serious face of a girl whom he had seen only once before in his life, and that was when she rode past the boundary-rider's hut with Leonie Linton and Harold a few days earlier. But though he had seen her only once, her likeness had printed itself on his memory as ineffaceably as the picture that is printed on a photographic plate by one brief instant's exposure to the sunlight.

"What has happened?" whispered Humphry, gazing up at clear grey eyes that looked down at him from under a coronet of golden-brown hair.

"Hush," said the girl. "You have had a fall. I was riding past and I found you lying on the ground. You will soon be all right. You were only stunned."

Humphry's head was lying in the girl's lap. She was sitting on the ground in her riding-habit, and there was a grey pony cropping the grass beside old Wallaroo, who was little the worse for his tumble. He had turned a half-somersault, falling on his back, as the condition of the big stock-saddle showed. The cross-tree in front was completely crushed, both knee-pads were broken, and the leather seat was split right across.

"You had a narrow escape," said the girl. "I was afraid at first that you were dead. However, I felt your heart and found that it was beating, so I went to the creek, soaked my handkerchief with water, and gave you a good douche. You soon came round."

"Thank you ever so much," said Humphry. "You probably saved my life. I saw you yesterday with Miss Linton, and now won't you tell me who you are?"

The girl gave a start and looked hard at Humphry. "My name is Marion Bingham," she said, "and I am staying at Yarralla, on a visit with the Lintons. When I saw you at first, stretched out on the ground, I thought you were Harold Hesseltine; but now, looking at you closely, I can see that I was mistaken. But the likeness is truly extraordinary."

The girl was puzzled and excited, and as she looked at the darkly handsome face and curling hair of the man who sat beside her, a sudden wave of emotion sent a rich flush of colour to cheek and neck.

"Won't you tell me who you are?" she said.

And Humphry answered simply, "I am the new boundary-rider."

CHAPTER X

THE MISUNDERSTANDING OF MARION

The law of gravitation which Newton discovered is still seriously misunderstood, even by many people who consider themselves well educated. They are aware that they cannot throw a stone at a dog without bringing into operation the great principle that the brain of Newton discerned as holding the universe together, but they fail to understand that when two bodies of opposite sexes, but of similar tastes and likings, approach each other's orbits they are predestined to gravitate towards each other—unless some other body exercises a stronger counter-attraction upon either of them—just as surely as two and two make four.

It was in accordance with this general principle that the major continued to haunt the front verandah of the Mindaroona homestead, where Mrs. Hesseltine spent much of her time and a portion of her superabundant energy in doing quite unnecessary fancy work.

It was also in obedience to this great law that Finegan, who figured officially as assistant bookkeeper at Caringal, drifted across with increasing frequency to Mindaroona, where Jeanie McPherson still presided over the weekly wash.

The same harmonious law of nature caused Harold and Leonie to ride together on spring mornings through the wide paddocks, so that Harold could forget for a time the secret mystery of his birth and Leonie could banish from her mind the uneasiness which had been created by her lover's evident preoccupation.

And finally the splendid generalisation of the philosopher explained with scientific accuracy the frequent morning rides which Marion Bingham took in the direction of the new boundary-rider's hut.

Pomologists may note as a singular coincidence that the apple has played an astonishingly important part in influencing human destiny.

It was through looking at an apple that Eve deprived humanity of the joys of a perpetual horticultural existence.

It was also through looking at an apple that Newton discovered the law which holds the planets in their places—and which caused this conjunction of different pairs of people at Mindaroona, Yarralla, and Caringal.

While Leonie was out riding with Harold, Marion was thrown a great deal upon her own resources, for Mrs. Linton seldom went far from the house, and found sufficient exercise in talking. She was a shrewd matron, and very observant, in spite of her chronic ill-health.

"My dear Marion," she said, in answer to some commiserating observations, "while Nature has given me a wretchedly weak back she has developed my tongue in compensation. As you have only lately left Madame Nichette's, I suppose you haven't yet forgotten Cuvier's law of correlation. When the horse lost his toes he acquired additional molars, you know. And the huge development of the lower jaw of the ape has been replaced in man by an enlargement of the brain-case. That's how it is, no doubt, that my organs of speech have become so vigorous. It was at the expense of my poor back. Now run along, dear, and try to amuse yourself till lunch-time."

So Marion went off for a solitary ride, and quite unconsciously, no doubt, took the track towards the boundary fence between Yarralla and Mindaroona. In the angle on the Mindaroona side was the boundary-rider's hut.

Humphry was sitting on a stump near his hut mending the stock-saddle that came to grief when the chestnut turned over. When he saw the girl on the grey pony, he let down the slip panel quickly, and welcomed his visitor with a bright smile.

"I hope you won't think me an intruder," said the girl, "but I have come to see how you are after that terrible crumpler near the creek."

She looked him straight in the eyes with her clear level gaze, and he experienced a new thrill of satisfaction as he realised the strength and sincerity of the girl's nature. Here were no wiles and subterfuges of sophisticated femininity. Fearless, straight-forward, and direct, Marion Bingham stood before him like a young Diana.

"Thank you ever so much for coming, Miss Bingham. I'm feeling splendid. Won't you get off the pony for a few minutes?"

The girl slipped easily from the saddle, hung the bridle over a fence-post, and sat down on the log. "Please don't think me rude," she said, "but you haven't even told me your name yet. Won't you tell it to me?"

"I am called Humphry Robertson," said the young man.

The girl was plainly puzzled. "But surely you must be related to Mr. Harold Hesseltine," said Marion, with those clear grey eyes searching his own with a serene confidence that made equivocation on his part impossible.

"It's a strange story, Miss Bingham, but you have done so much for me already that I feel I ought to tell you. If it hadn't been for your kindly aid I should probably have had a bad time out there by the creek."

Marion Bingham laid her hand lightly on the boundary-rider's arm. "Mr. Robertson," she said, "please don't think that I want to pry into your private affairs. I have no such desire, I assure you. But my dearest girl-friend, Miss Linton, is engaged to Harold Hesseltine, and you are so astonishingly like him that you might easily be — what shall I say? — his twin brother."

And then he told her.

Marion listened with wide-eyed interest to the bare recital of unvarnished facts. "Please believe that I am truly sorry for you, Mr. Robertson," she said, "but I feel certain that your search will be successful. Something in your face tells me that you will go on until you find her. Of course, I knew at once that you were not an ordinary boundary-rider." And then she added, with naive and charming seriousness, "I am very glad indeed that I have met you. I should like you to understand how deeply I sympathise with you."

"Miss Bingham," said Humphry quietly, "you don't know how much you have done for me by giving me your friendship. I am sure it is not necessary to ask you to keep silence about all that I have told you, so I will merely say that if my identity and my presence here were guessed it would spoil everything. If Mrs. Hesseltine or Major McLean, or even Miss Linton, were to see me, it would be fatal to the success of the inquiries which I am trying to make here among the old servants of Mr. Hesseltine concerning the events that followed Mrs. Hesseltine's return from Melbourne with that baby who was my brother Harold."

"But how have you escaped being discovered already?" asked Marion wonderingly.

"Every one who sees me takes me for Harold," said Humphry, "but I dare not risk a meeting with Mrs. Hesseltine or the major. Either of them would be sure to detect the difference between us. So I will ask you not to say anything to anybody about me, not even to Miss Linton, until I have found my mother—alive or dead."

Marion Bingham held out her hand with a sudden impulse. "You have my promise," she said, "as well as my sympathy."

Humphry took the offered hand and pressed it in silence.

"And you must let me ride over and see you quite often," said Marion, "for you have made me almost as anxious as you are yourself to penetrate the mystery. I am anxious for Harold's sake— and for Leonie's, as well as for yours. And now, goodbye."

She mounted the grey pony and cantered off towards Yarralla, while Humphry watched her with his hand shading his eyes from the midday glare.

But as Marion cantered away from the hut she carried in her heart a new feeling of interest for the man who had trusted her with his strange secret. She realised that she now had the grave responsibility of guarding Humphry's confidence and keeping it even from the knowledge of Leonie, with whom she had hitherto shared her inmost thoughts.

With her high ideals of life and her steadfast resolution to seek her own happiness by achieving happiness for others, Marion's feeling for pretty pleasure-loving, easily influenced Leonie was almost maternal. She wished above all things to see Leonie really happy. Thus she had encouraged Leonie to talk freely to her about Harold, and had listened with indulgent interest to all the details of Harold's wooing. Leonie had told her about her lover's preoccupation and strange silences ever since that afternoon in the ironworks at Shaleville.

And Leonie was evidently seriously put out about it.

"Of course, you can't understand how I feel about it, Marion," Leonie had said, "because you are so strong and self-contained. And you have never been in love yourself."

Was that careless remark still true? Marion asked herself. There was a new light in her eyes as she cantered back to Yarralla. But she felt genuinely grieved that she was pledged to say nothing to Leonie about the boundary-rider who was Harold's brother. Concerning this new and splendid thing that had come into her life she was bound to maintain strict silence.

It was the first time during her long friendship with Leonie that she had kept a single secret from her.

A mile from the homestead Marion met Harold and Leonie riding side by side.

Leonie called to her affectionately: "Come along, Marion, we have been looking for you everywhere," and as Marion rode up she whispered to her, "Harold is so silent and moody, dear, that I'm thankful you've come. I cannot think what has come over him. He's not a bit loving to-day, and I simply must be loved. I can't live without it. Why, I lost him this morning for more than half an hour, and goodness knows where he got to. He doesn't seem to know himself."

Marion gave her an affectionate smile. "You needn't be a bit alarmed, dear," she said. "Nobody could leave off loving you, if they tried. Could they, Harold?"

"Of course not," said Harold, emerging for a moment from introspective gloom. "And certainly I am not going to try, Leonie, so you needn't expect it." His face wore a sunny smile again, even if it was an evanescent one.

"Why, you dear old thing, you'll make me positively jealous," said Leonie, pulling her cob alongside Marion's grey pony. "Directly you join us Harold forgets his secret sorrows—I'm sure he must have some secret sorrows, by the way that he behaves—and gets quite bright again." The gay little butterfly flitted on and on—fluttering her wings over hidden fires. Life had dealt very kindly with Leonie until lately, when some mysterious shadow had come between her and her lover.

She joked about it. She rallied him upon his moodiness and preoccupation, but the thought of it came back to her like a grisly visitant in the night watches. What was the cause of Harold's changed manner? She felt in her soul that he was not giving her his confidence, and the depths beneath her superficial gaiety were troubled.

The same night, when the two girls were preparing for bed in the big double bedroom which they shared at Yarralla, Leonie became inquisitive.

"Where did you ride to this morning, dear?"

The question came like a shot out of a gun, and Marion, startled out of her day-dreaming, could only stammer: "Just across the paddocks to the boundary fence."

The big double bedroom at Yarralla contained two beds, each hung with snowy mosquito curtains. It also contained two dressing-tables and one large double wardrobe with looking-glass doors. It is necessary that the position of these various articles of furniture should be stated in order that it may be understood how it was that Leonie Linton found out that Marion Bingham, whom she had always regarded as the soul of honour, and to whom she had given all her confidence, was deceiving her.

At the end of the left-hand wall, then, as one entered the room was the door, and against the centre of the same wall was placed Marion's dressing-table.

Leonie's dressing-table stood across the angle formed by the right-hand wall and the lower end-wall. The centre of the upper end-wall was occupied by the large wardrobe with looking-glass doors.

The effect of this quite fortuitous arrangement was that when the right-hand door of the wardrobe was left a few inches open a person sitting in front of Leonie's dressing-table could see a person sitting in front of Marion's dressing-table reflected in profile in the slightly opened looking-glass door of the wardrobe, although the two persons were at the time sitting almost back to back.

This was the position when Leonie, in night-gown and dainty be-ribboned wrapper, sat in front of her own dressing-table doing her hair preparatory to retiring for the night, while Marion in a very similar costume was performing identical rites in front of the other dressing-table.

"I hope you are not being awfully bored by being left by yourself so much, you poor old dear," resumed Leonie, brushing out her beautiful mane of gold-shot hair with a sideways sweep of the elaborate silver-backed brush and a dexterous flick to disengage the ends as she finished each stroke.

"Not a bit," cheerfully said Marion, who was going through the same graceful process at her side of the room.

"Because I wanted to say such a lot of things to Harold," continued the daughter of the house sentimentally, "and yet when we were alone together he was so silent and reserved that I could hardly find anything to say at all. Isn't it strange?"

Marion expressed the opinion with her lips that it was rather strange, but in her heart she admitted to herself that the secret which Harold shared with Humphry concerning their parentage was quite sufficient to make anybody absent-minded.

"How did the pony carry you, dear?" went on Leonie, who was in a decidedly talkative mood and always enjoyed this half-hour of chatter over the events of the day with her particular chum.

"Splendidly!" said Marion with enthusiasm. "He's a perfect little hack, and I like him because it's so easy to get on him again, you know, after one has dismounted."

"Oh, so you got off him to-day while you were out, did you, dear?" Leonie finished the brushing process and began methodically to plait her lovely hair into two long pigtails.

"Yes," said Marion rather abruptly, "I did."

"What for?" inquired Leonie; "there were no gates to open, were there?"

"No, there were not," said Marion. "I wanted to talk to

somebody. By the way, have you seen the major lately? That strange creature Finegan told me that the major was dreadfully upset by that Indian hawker who told him his fortune."

Leonie finished one pigtail and began the other without speaking. This violent changing of the subject was unlike Marion. Surely there was no need to make a mystery about her morning ride. "You didn't tell me that you met anybody when you were out," she said with just a tinge of reproachfulness in her voice.

"Didn't I?"

"No, you didn't. Who was it?"

"Oh, nobody of any consequence. Let's ride across to the Black Mountain in the morning, Leonie, and boil a billy at the shepherd's hut. There's a lovely view of the sea from the top of the hill."

"Marion, I do believe you're keeping something back from me. You seem quite different to-night."

"Do I, dear?" Marion was busy with her own pigtail now, but her hands were shaking so that she could hardly make the three-ply plait. She managed, however, to finish the plait, and it was the second one. With a quick twist or two she tied up the end of it and both pigtails hung down completed.

Marion pushed back her chair, stood up, and taking her skirt from the foot of her bed, opened the right-hand looking-glass door of the wardrobe and hung the skirt on a hook inside.

Then she closed the door.

But she did not close it carefully and it swung open again, just a little—only about three inches, in fact. Still, like Mercutio's wound, it would do.

When Marion sat down again in front of her dressing-table to finish doing her hair, the looking-glass door of the wardrobe stood slightly open, bringing the plane of the mirror into an angle where it caught the reflection of the unconscious sitter and projected it upon the reflection of the wardrobe-door seen in Leonie's dressing-table mirror.

Leonie, as she coiled her own plaits over her head and tied them in a knot at the back, could see in her own mirror the girl who sat back to back with her performing exactly the same pretty toilet manoeuvre. Marion's face showed out with lifelike distinctness.

"Marion dear, you haven't told me yet who it was that you met this morning."

Marion laughed a little awkwardly. "You shouldn't be so inquisitive, Leonie," she said; "it's very bad for you."

Leonie elevated her pretty nose ever so little. "Really, Marion," she said, with just a suspicion of coolness in her voice, "one might think from all this mystery that you were in love with him."

That was the shot that did the mischief.

A rich deep flush of colour rose in Marion's pale cheek and covered her face, spreading downwards over the snowy neck and upwards to where the soft brown hair came to meet the broad and well-shaped forehead.

And Leonie, gazing petrified into her looking-glass, saw the signal hoisted which showed her that firing at random she had scored a bull's-eye.

"Marion!" The word escaped from her lips almost without her knowledge, as she turned, crossed the room in a few swift steps, and stared into her friend's face.

The flush died down as quickly as it came and left Marion paler than before.

"And you never told me, Marion. You, who have had no secrets from me until now. What does it mean?"

"You must not ask me, Leonie, for I cannot tell you," said Marion, mistress of herself again with a mighty effort.

"Not tell me!" said Leonie, in amazement; "won't you tell me what his name is?"

And Marion, looking at her straight in the eyes with that direct unfaltering gaze of hers, made answer: "No."

"Oh, very well," said Leonie shortly; "good-night." And without another word she lifted the mosquito curtains, crept into her bed, and turned her face to the wall.

"Good-night, Leonie," said Marion quietly. "I'm very sorry that you are offended, but it's really not my fault."

She put out the lights one by one and crept into her own bed—but not to sleep. The incidents of the day had been too exciting, and she had much to think about.

As for Leonie, that unhappy damsel was even more wakeful than Marion.

One question hammered ceaselessly in her brain.

Where was Harold during the time that he was absent from her on their morning ride?

CHAPTER XI

A FANCIED TREASON

Next morning Leonie felt calmer and a little ashamed of her outburst of temper. It was simply inconceivable that her dark suspicion of the previous evening could have any foundation. She was engaged to marry Harold, and Marion was her closest friend. How, then, could there be anything between Marion and Harold?

No reference was made by either of the girls to the episode of the night before, and Leonie was determinedly cheerful and cordial. The serene and fearless frankness of Marion, conscious that she had been guilty of no treachery to her friend, and quite at a loss to account for Leonie's display of anger, was unchanged.

Breakfast passed off quite satisfactorily, Mrs. Linton doing most of the talking, and then the three ladies separated, the elder lady betaking herself to the morning-room to meet Mr. Grist, the station manager, and hear his report of the lambing, while the two younger ones busied themselves about the house.

Leonie was quite amiable again, but still at the bottom of her mind lay the unsolved puzzle, like an ugly snag fallen into a clear pool. She could not help wondering why Marion refused to tell her who it was that she met during her solitary morning ride.

She was looking out of the drawing-room window across the well-grassed Yarralla paddocks towards the rounded hump of Black Mountain in the distance, when her ear caught the soft rhythm of cantering hoofs, and, turning her head, she saw Harold riding his favourite hack, old Hailstorm.

Leonie's face brightened. She waved her handkerchief from the window. Soon she would be able to see through the mystery. Harold would clear up all her doubts.

But unhappily Harold did not see the fluttering handkerchief. He made no answering signal. He rode right up to the gate, slipped off his horse—and shook hands with Marion, who had gone out to meet him.

Leonie felt as though an invisible hand had clutched her by the throat. Furious with rage, she saw Marion talking rapidly and earnestly to Harold. She saw her place her hand on Harold's arm and walk away with him down the garden, while Harold listened to her eagerly, and at intervals looked round nervously to see if any one was watching them.

What could those two be talking about? What secret were they keeping from her?

Leonie was tormented by jealousy. She picked up a book and tried to read, but her vagrant thoughts refused to be controlled, and she could not concentrate her attention on the pages. She could not even sit still in the chair, but kept feverishly running to the window to see whether her dearest girl-friend and her affianced lover had yet returned from their conference.

After at least a quarter of an hour of waiting she saw them come back into view. Marion held out her hand at the gate. Harold grasped it and held it for several seconds. He seemed to be deeply moved as he listened to what Marion was saying. At last he lifted Hailstorm's bridle off the hook in the gate-post, and mounted and rode away.

Not a word for Leonie!

He had ridden over to Yarralla; Marion had intercepted him, and then he had ridden away. Was there any possible explanation of that conduct—except the obvious one?

Leonie sat down and tried to collect her thoughts, but she was like a person stunned by a sudden blow. Gradually her single impulse reasserted itself. She would go and find Marion. She would speak to her calmly but firmly—oh yes, very calmly. There must be some simple explanation of all that she had seen, and Marion, of course, would give it to her.

Stirred to the unknown deeps that lie beneath even the shallowest feminine soul when the primeval mating instinct is insulted and outraged, Leonie ran out of the house to look for Marion.

But Marion was not there, and the grey pony's stall was empty in the stable.

Larry, the rouseabout, who was smoking a short clay pipe while he washed a buggy, was able to supply some useful information, though it took him some time to do it.

"Arrah, Miss Leonie, shure 'tis only a few minnits agone since Miss Marion she come up to me in a therrible hurry, and she sez, 'Larry,' sez she, 'I want ye to saddle the powny for me at wanst,' sez she, "cause 'tis a matther uv importhance,' sez she, 'an' I can't be waitin',' sez she."

"Yes, yes. Go on, go on!"

"An' I sez to her, 'Miss Marion,' sez I, 'shure 'tis yerself is the rale lady,' sez I, 'an' let alone put the saddle on the powny for ye,' sez I, 'shure I'd walk to the great cross uv Croagh Patrick on me knees an' back for ye,' sez I, 'if ye axed me,' sez I, and wid that— — —-"

"Stop, stop, Larry, for Heaven's sake! Tell me where she went."

"An' wid that I put the ould saddle on the powny, Miss Leonie, because the new wan'll be givin' him a sore back be rason uv Miss Marion settin' too much over on the near side, an' I buckled them girts as tight as I cud, Miss Leonie, bekase that grey powny is as cunnin' as the divil, savin' yer presince, miss, an' he do be blowin' himsilf out whin I puts the girts round him, so as it's harrd wurruk to fix him at all, at all. So I just buckles thim girts as tight as I can, miss, and then in a minnit or two, whin he ain't thinkin' about it, I buckles thim a bit tighter."

"Well, well! which way did she go?"

"Shure I lifted her into the saddle, miss, an' she put her fut in the palm uv me hand an' wint up as aisy as a burrd, God bless her! and then she sez to me, 'Larry,' sez she— —"

"Larry, you'll drive me mad! Which track did she take?" Leonie stamped her pretty foot, and the flood of Larry's loquacity was stayed.

"She tuk the thrack to Mindaroona, miss," said Larry, a trifle sulkily. He enjoyed hearing himself talk, and disliked to be rudely interrupted. "She axed me how fur it is to the boundary-rider's hut, an' I tould her 'twas a matther uv five miles."

Leonie was already leading out her own horse, Tim, who stood in his stall already saddled. Larry held his horny palm for her foot, and she dropped into the saddle with practised ease.

"The saints presarve us!" ejaculated Larry as he looked with eyes shaded by levelled palm at a light cloud of dust travelling swiftly along the track to Mindaroona. "If Tim puts his fut in a crab-hole goin' at that pace, shure he'll t'row Miss Leonie from here inter Queensland."

But Tim knew enough to keep out of crab-holes, and with a light weight in the saddle he thoroughly enjoyed a fast gallop.

As Leonie topped the last rise and came in sight of the dividing fence between Yarralla and Mindaroona she saw the grey pony tied up to the fence near the boundary-rider's hut on the Mindaroona side. But there was no sign of Marion.

She pulled Tim into a trot, and making a wide turn, steered for a slip panel half a mile away from the hut. Passing into the Mindaroona paddock, she rode up the gently rising slope in a half circle that brought her to within a hundred yards of the back of the boundary-rider's home. There she slipped down from her saddle and tied Tim to a tree.

Gathering up her riding-skirt, she walked quickly and resolutely towards the hut. There were no signs of any human occupants, but the grey pony tied to a fence-post was conclusive proof that Marion was not far away.

Leonie clenched her teeth. So frank, fearless Marion, with her high ideals of life, her desire to find happiness by helping others to be happy, and her disinterested devotion to her school friend of earlier days, was in that hut.

Presumably she was not alone there. Leonie's breathing quickened and her heart beat faster as her thoughts framed the unspoken question: "Who was in the boundary-rider's hut with Marion?"

With all her lighthearted gaiety that merged at times into sheer frivolity, Leonie was an honourable girl to whom eavesdropping in her normal mood was as repugnant as any other kind of treachery. If any one had told her twenty-four hours earlier that she would act the part of a spy, and especially of a spy upon the actions of Marion, she would have repelled the statement with bitter indignation.

Yet here she was—creeping through the light scrub that stood behind the boundary-rider's hut, with one idea in her head and only one, namely, to see with her own eyes who it was that her frank and open-hearted friend, who had never before had any secrets from her, went to meet in this surreptitious way.

A woman deceived in her love is a woman transformed. The girl who made her way noiselessly and bending low through the young saplings and the patches of lantana was not the real Leonie, joyous, gay, and happy, but a frenzied 'double' with close-pressed lips and staring eyes, intent only on unmasking a deceiver.

She was certain that she would find Marion in the hut, but she hardly dared to think who was Marion's companion—if she had one.

Coming within the last twenty yards of the hut, Leonie dropped on her hands and knees and crawled through the long grass lest the occupants of the hut, whoever they were, should see her through the little square window cut in the centre of the wall.

Then she heard voices, and held her breath to listen. She was quite close up to the wall now. It was Marion who was speaking.

"Leonie must not know," said the voice of Marion inside the hut, "it would be such a terrible shock to her to find that the man she loves is not what he seems to be."

And then another voice, a man's voice with a strangely familiar intonation, said: "Poor little Leonie! I can't help feeling sorry for her. We must keep it from her at all costs, not only for her sake, but for ours."

The girl listening outside amid the long grass and the undergrowth caught at her heart with a sudden spasm of pain. She had never imagined that such treachery as this could exist on earth.

"She seemed to suspect something last night," said the voice of Marion again. "She asked me who it was that I had met in the morning when I was out riding."

"And what did you tell her?" said the man's voice anxiously.

"I refused to tell her anything at all," said Marion's voice, "because I would not tell her an untruth and I could not tell her that it was you."

Leonie crawled a few paces nearer to the hut through the brushwood and the tall stems of grass. She behaved like a person who is hypnotised. She advanced as though under the compulsion of some hidden and mysterious force.

With restless gaze she hastily examined the end wall of the hut, and soon she found what she was looking for—a knot-hole in the timber. It was a couple of feet above the level of the ground and commanded the whole interior of the little structure.

Placing her right eye to the knot-hole, Leonie, who was still on her hands and knees, peeped into the hut.

A rough bunk covered with a blue blanket, two wooden chairs and a small table, a few pictures of racehorses cut from illustrated papers and pasted on the wall—that was all there was in the way of furniture and decoration.

A man and a woman were sitting on the two chairs close to each other. The woman was Marion, but the watcher outside could not see the man's face. It was turned away from her. She saw that he was dressed in coat and trousers of rough tweed, and that he wore leggings and spurs.

The man was holding Marion's hand in his, and as she noted his slim figure a horrible conviction grew in the mind of the eavesdropper.

"You are right," he said, "Leonie must never know."

As he uttered the words he turned half way round in the chair and Leonie saw his features—the features of Harold, the man to whom she was betrothed!

She neither screamed nor sobbed. No cry of pain escaped her, but her face was deathly white as she staggered back to the tree where she had left her horse. Leading Tim to a stump, she mounted him like a woman in a dream, and Tim carried her safely home.

But when Marion returned she was met by Larry, the rouseabout, with serious news. "She wint out on Tim here to find ye, miss, an' be this an' be that whin she come home agin an hour agone she looked for all the wurruld like a shtone image, an' the eyes uv her shtarin' shtraight t'roo me, as if I wuz a bit uv windy-glass, an' the tongue uv her sayin' divil a wurrud. But she slid down off the harrse an' she wint inter the house like as if she wuz walkin' in her shlape. The saints presarve us, miss! fwat did ye be doin' to poor Miss Leonie at all at all?"

But Marion did not wait to explain. A chill premonition swept over her, for with lightning-like intuition she conjectured what had happened. Leonie by some means or other had seen her in the hut with Humphry, and had mistaken him for Harold.

Marion flew to the house and met Mrs. Linton in the doorway. The elder lady was shaken for once out of her self-possession. She clutched Marion fiercely by the arm. "What have you been doing to my child?" she said. And then both women paused and looked at each other with horror-stricken eyes, for a dreadful moaning came to them from the drawing-room, where stretched on the sofa lay poor Leonie 'a-babbling o' green fields.

The doctor who came out from Shaleville the same afternoon shook his head ominously. "It's brain," he said; "the poor child must have had a shock of some kind."

So Marion was installed as nurse and the horror of a great fear came down upon Yarralla.

But Humphry when he heard of it took a hopeful view. "It all hangs together as part of the same trouble," he said to Harold, who had ridden out to him for comfort in his grief and fear. "It seems as though the unquiet spirit of our mother is still at work. When I find her, as surely I shall, then every perplexity will be cleared up and you will get your Leonie back safe and sound again."

Harold shook his head sorrowfully. It was a forlorn hope.

CHAPTER XII

THE WRECK AT BLACKFISH BAY

"Oh, stop yer haverin', mon, for A hae ma claes to pit oot on the line an' the win's blowin' them down as fast as A can pit them oot."

Jeanie McPherson was wrestling heroically with her wash, and it in no way assisted her to have the society of Tim Finegan during the process, especially as Finegan persisted in putting his arm round her waist at the precise moment when she was unable to protect herself.

When a sonsie lassie is holding down a wire clothes-line with one hand and affixing a newly washed undergarment to it by means of wooden pegs with the other, and when, moreover, she is obliged to stand on tiptoe in order to reach the line, how can she prevent an active and enterprising fellow from snatching a hurried embrace?

Jeanie found it impossible. But she could at least make reprisals, as Finegan found when he received a ringing box on the ear from the exasperated damsel.

"Hae done wi' yer fulin'," snapped Jeanie; "canna ye see that the win's rising an' a' the claes will be ower the fence if A canna get them pinned doun richt sune."

And indeed the drying-ground was already whitened as though with newly fallen snow. Garments of divers shapes were whirled about by the advance gusts of the coming storm, and Jeanie in hot pursuit darted hither and thither after them, intent on anchoring them securely before worse things happened.

Finegan lent a hand, and his assistance, though awkward, was timely, so that Jeanie surveyed the situation with the satisfaction of a skipper who sees, when the barometer is tumbling fast and the gale to windward is rapidly approaching, that his

110

royals and t'gallants'ls are down and his upper tops'ls double-reefed.

It took more than an insincere box on the ears to stop Finegan when he was on a combined mission of courtship and investigation.

He proceeded with his cross-examination pertinaciously.

"How has Mr. Harold been spending his time lately, Jeanie?"

"A dinna ken, A'm sure," replied the damsel; "but the puir laddie's amaist daft wi' the trouble up at Yarralla. I heard the mestress tellin' the major that puir Miss Leonie raves awfu' aboot Mesther Harold. She lees there a' day lang movin' her han's restless-like on the counterpin an' sayin' naethin' but 'He's broke ma hairt! He's broke ma hairt!'"

Poor Jeanie was quite affected, and she dashed a tear or two hastily from her eyes.

Finegan was interested in Leonie's illness merely as a side issue. It was evidently connected in some way with the association between Harold and Humphry, but the inquiry agent sheered off instinctively to more solid ground.

"Do you know what Mr. Harold has been doing, Jeanie? Where has he been and who has he seen?"

"Angus McPhee was in last nicht," said Jeanie with an air of mystery. "Him and me is frae the same toun, ye ken."

"Well, what did he tell you?"

"A daurna say."

"Oh, come along now, Jeanie! I really want to know."

"Weel, tak yer airm frae roun' ma waist first. There, that's better noo. Weel, Angus McPhee tellt me that Mesther Harold rode ower the Black Mountain to see him last Thursday."

"Ah!"

"An' stayed there haverin' wi' him for best pairt of an oor."

"Um. What did he want to know?"

"Mesther McPhee tellt me that Mesther Harold showed him a photygraf."

"Yes, yes. Who was it?"

"'Twas a photygraf of a wumman."

"What sort of a woman, Jeanie? What did she look like?"

Finegan felt that he was on a trail of some sort. He, too, was looking for traces of a woman.

"Angus tellt me 'twas a verra bonnie leddy. Mesther Harold was speirin' aboot the leddy. He asked Angus did he remember ever seein' her at Mindaroona."

Here was mystification, indeed, for Finegan.

The lady that Harold was looking for could hardly be the lady that the major was looking for surely. Who was Harold's lady, anyhow, and why should he expect that McPhee might remember her? Finegan realised that these were questions that must be answered.

"Well, Jeanie lass, I'll not keep you from your work any longer this morning. I must be going back to the store now." Finegan reached for his hat.

"Gude-bye, Mesther Finegan," said Jeanie, and then she added coyly as an afterthought: "A didna mean tae hurt ye wi' that bit slap i' the lug."

So she got another embrace and there was no slap after it. "Ye can come again if ye like the morn's morn," said Jeanie, as Finegan climbed up on the quiet old stock-horse that had carried him across to Mindaroona from Caringal.

Finegan set off at a sober jog towards the Black Mountain, purposing to interview McPhee about that photograph. The wind that had played with Jeanie's washing had freshened fast and was now blowing hard from the south. Finegan had a very disagreeable ride to Angus McPhee's camp and he was glad when it was over.

The old Scotchman was at first very suspicious and disinclined to talk to the new bookkeeper from Caringal, but under the mollifying influence of a large plug of tobacco that Finegan presented him with he gradually found his tongue and described in his own picturesque Doric the visit that he had received from 'Mesther Harold.'

Mr. McPhee, who was great on detail and never forgot anything, even mentioned the curious fact that Jess, the collie, who had known Harold since she was a pup, sniffed and growled at him, and persisted in regarding him as a stranger.

Finegan pricked up his ears at once. Was it possible that it was not Harold who visited the old man and asked about the photograph but Harold's double, the young ironworker, who had been conferring with Harold at the 'Miners' Rest,' and who disappeared after that fearful experience on the top of the blast furnace? There seemed to be no end to the terrible tangle of possibilities, but as he sat on the log outside McPhee's hut talking to the old shepherd, Finegan realised in a flash one of the possibilities, if not even one of the probabilities.

Harold Hesseltine and Humphry Robertson, alias Scott, who were as like each other as two new pennies, were working together in order to find traces of a certain woman. One of them—he did not know which—had gone to Angus McPhee for information and had questioned him about events dating twenty years back and about an unknown woman's movements at that distant date. Major McLean was also seeking for information about a woman's movements twenty years ago. The major's advertisements in the Melbourne papers had produced no result, a fact which indicated to Mr. Finegan that the persons who could give the information must have some strong reason for withholding it. Why should they withhold it—and thereby lose the reward of fifty pounds—unless they feared to get into trouble by giving it? It seemed probable, therefore, that the missing woman had at least committed some irregularity and that the person at whose house she stayed in Melbourne was mixed up in it.

Finegan's brain was not particularly acute naturally, but it had had plenty of practice in dealing with the motives of people who disappeared from their accustomed haunts. He followed the trail fairly closely for some distance, but finally fell into the common mistake of forming a theory and trying to make the facts fit it, instead of ascertaining enough facts first to substitute deduction for hypothesis.

It seemed to the private inquiry agent that the missing woman had obtained money from some person by false pretences and that the boarding-house keeper—a woman, of course—had instigated the plan and shared in the plunder. Hence the disappearance of the principal and the profound silence of the accessory.

Finegan resolved to place his theory before the major and suggest a trip for himself to Melbourne in order to hunt up that accessory. He was convinced that he would be able to find her.

All this passed through his brain as he sat on the log, when a sharp cry from McPhee made him look up. Whew! it was blowing a hard gale now and the sea was obscured by frequent squalls.

"Man, man, look at yon steamer!" shouted McPhee through the whistle of the gale, and facing round to the sea, Finegan made out through the flying drift a large steamer perilously close inshore.

She was quite out of control and was fast coming in, broadside on, straight towards the Walrus Rock. At times, lifted high on a big sea, she rolled until she showed half her keel, and then, diving into a hollow, seemed as though she could never come up again.

"She's lost her propeller," shouted Finegan to old McPhee. "She'll be on the rocks in half-an-hour. You had better go down to the beach, McPhee, and see if you can do anything, while I ride back and stir up the men at Mindaroona, Caringal, and Yarralla."

The news that a large steamer was in difficulties and likely to go ashore spread through the district incredibly quickly, and Finegan, when halfway back to Caringal, met the major with a buggy full of blankets and medical comforts on his way to the beach.

"Come along, Finegan," shouted the major "no time to lose," and the buggy was off again at a hand gallop, as Finegan turned the old stock-horse round and joined in the race.

It was a wild helter-skelter, typically Australian in character, the stampede of a whole district that may be seen commonly after a country race-meeting and less frequently at a shipwreck.

Every man, woman, and child who could climb on a horse or squeeze into a buggy was flying along the wide stock road as if his or her arrival first upon the scene was essential to the safety of every soul on board the vessel.

Finegan took a good pull at the old stock-horse, but with very little effect, for the excitement of the chase had come over the veteran and he was going much faster than the rider liked. The stock-horse tore at the bit and went even faster as Larry, the rouseabout, with a wild "Hurroo!" went past on poor Leonie's favourite hack, Tim, flinging lumps of mud from the horse's flying heels in the face of the luckless inquiry agent.

Every bush hand from the three stations had joined in the rush, and every cocky from the surrounding district. They bumped, jostled, challenged each other, and raced towards the sea, while the gale that swept inland from the coast was laden with spindrift, discordant yells, and clods of earth thrown back by the galloping hoofs, so that those at the rear of the procession had anything but an enjoyable time. A white-haired bush parson in his sulky kept close beside Finegan, evidently determined that if his services were required they should be available, and the local medical man whizzed past them on his motor-cycle, conjecturing with plenty of reason that it would be strange if he could not find a few patients before the day was over.

And then Finegan became aware of a big horse overhauling him fast on the near side and going with a long easy stride that the old stock-horse, with his short stiff, proppy action, could not hope to keep pace with. It was Wallaroo, the chestnut, and to his amazement Finegan saw that the rider was none other than Humphry Robertson, the missing double of Harold Hesseltine. Finegan knew by the rider's rough bush clothes that he was not the immaculate young heir of Mindaroona.

Here was a discovery. But the inquiry agent at once resolved to keep it to himself. Whoever Robertson might be, at least he had saved Finegan's life at the imminent peril of his own. Finegan experienced the same creepy chill down his spine that always returned when he thought of that night above the blast furnace. In common decency he could not give Humphry Robertson away to the major, who would certainly insist on probing his mysterious connection with Harold and his extraordinary resemblance to that young man to the bottom.

The major reached the beach in front of Finegan, and just as

115

he got there a cry of dismay went up from the spectators gathered on the edge of the little bay.

The big steamer heaved up her side on a huge roller and came down with a crash on the Walrus Rock, over which the broken water was foaming.

The major pulled out a pocket telescope and examined her closely. "I can just make out the name on her bows," he said to the medical motor-cyclist, who stood beside him. "She's the Goorabinda, of the White Anchor Line, with passengers and cargo for Queensland ports."

Major McLean rested his telescope on the doctor's shoulder and made a prolonged examination of the wreck. Walrus Rock was a little more than two miles from the reefs at the southern end of the bay, and a good three miles from the sandy beach where the crowd of spectators had gathered, this being the only spot where the boats could effect a landing.

"She's lying over at a fearful angle to the port side," reported the major, "and the seas are breaking right over her waist, but she has gone head on to the reef, and if she doesn't slip off and sink in deep water they ought to be able to get the boats out."

The people on the sandy beach could see with the naked eye the clouds of white foam and spray that dashed mast-high over the doomed ship. At times nothing was visible but the funnel and the two masts as an unusually big sea swept over her.

"Hullo! they're trying to get the life-boats out on the port side!" exclaimed the major. "She has such a list to port that it is impossible to launch the starboard boats. Not many people on board apparently."

Minutes elapsed—minutes full of extreme tension for the onlookers, who were powerless to give any assistance. But all at once a cheer rang out, telling of relief from the pentup anxiety. The crowd had seen a boat successfully launched.

"Yes, it's all right," said the major excitedly, with his eye glued to the telescope; "they're pulling away from the ship. I can see another boat being launched on the port side near the stern, where the ship makes a lee-side for it. There it goes into the water. By

George, nearly over that time! Now then, the question is whether the two boats can live through such a heavy sea to reach the shore."

The progress of the boats to the shore was painfully slow, but the people on the beach occupied the time under the major's direction in building several large fires of brushwood and driftwood for the benefit of the ship-wrecked unfortunates.

The major was so busy in superintending this operation that though he had, as he thought, seen Harold Hesseltine among the crowd he had no time to go and speak to him. And Humphry, on his side, was careful to keep away from the major as far as possible.

At last the deeply laden boats drew near to the shore, and as a heavy surf was rolling in, it needed careful handling to avoid a catastrophe even at the eleventh hour. But the mate, who was in charge of the first boat, knew his job, and so did the men at the oars. "Now, lads, give way!" shouted the mate, and as the men bent to their work the boat shot forward fairly on the crest of a gigantic roller that carried her forward with the speed of a railway train and ran her along until the bow touched the sand. Before the backwash could get hold of her a dozen of the stalwart fellows on the beach, including Humphry, had rushed into the water and dragged the boat well up into security.

Drenched and chilled, but happy to have escaped with their lives, the passengers, among whom were several women, and the sailors and firemen, who were exhausted with rowing, joined the onlookers on the beach in watching with breathless anxiety the landing of the captain's boat. The second boat was not so fortunate as the first, for she capsized in the surf, and though all the occupants were brought safe to shore by willing hands, they reached the beach at last in a half drowned condition.

Humphry had been through the surf half a dozen times on missions of rescue, and he was glad to creep to a place near one of the big fires round which all the shipwrecked people were gathered. Medical comforts from the major's buggy went round in tin pannikins, and presently one of the women passengers started a hymn, and the whole assemblage was soon engaged in singing with a lusty fervour that would have shamed many a congregation comfortably housed in church.

A careful investigation by Captain Black showed that not a single soul had been lost, although there was no hope of saving the vessel.

Captain Black was a grizzled old sea-dog who had been in command of the Goorabinda for nearly a score of years and had never had an accident before. He was heartbroken at the loss of his ship, and Humphry could get very little out of him.

"I've got to stand by the ship whatever happens," said Captain Black, but he would vouchsafe no reason, and Humphry was left under the impression that the captain's resolution was due to nothing more than the dogged determination of an old salt not to desert his shipwrecked vessel as long as she was still above water.

"D—d death-trap, that's what the Walrus Rock is," muttered Captain Black in Humphry's ear. "In an easterly gale there's a set of the tide into this bay that'll pull a ship miles out of her course even if nothing goes wrong with her engines. The old Goorabinda broke her tail-shaft just off Stingray Point, and I knew it was a case with us from the first. But it's a marvel to me that ships haven't been lost here before now. Next to King Island and the Three Kings off the New Zealand coast, it's the worst place I know of in these seas."

"Any chance of getting the Goorabinda off, captain?" asked Humphry.

"'Fraid not, young fellow; but I must borrow a buggy and get some one to drive me to the nearest telegraph office now. I expect you'll see a couple of tugs with Lloyd's agent aboard one of 'em round here by the morning."

Captain Black shut his lips tight and became uncommunicative as an oyster. Apparently he thought that he had said too much already.

Humphry strolled round the different fires and listened to the speculations of the shipwrecked sailors and passengers, most of whom had decided to camp there for the night with the available provisions and wait for the representatives of the steamship company to arrange to send them on to their various destinations.

"The captain seems very anxious to stay by the vessel," Humphry ventured to a loquacious fireman, who was flourishing a tin pannikin in which, alas! no more medical comforts remained.

"Sh'd think 'e would too," observed the fireman thickly, and then he gave a portentous wink designed to convey the most significant information. "There's specie aboard the old Goorabinda. Twenty thousand sovereigns consigned to one of the Brisbane banks. That's worth lookin' after, aint it? You'll see the bloomin' underwriters here by breakfast-time."

By this time it was nearly dark, the hymn-singing had ceased, and many of the passengers had wrapped themselves in the blankets that the major had brought down, and were trying to sleep beside the regularly replenished fires. Harold looked out towards the Walrus Rock, but his eyes could not pierce the darkness. He was vaguely conscious of a feeling that the Walrus Rock exercised some subtle influence over him. He found himself turning his gaze seaward again and again, but in vain.

The moon rose at ten o'clock, and at mid-night was riding high in the sky, making a broad pathway of light along the tumbling water. Humphry woke from a doze, and again unconsciously his gaze turned seaward towards the reef.

He rubbed his eyes incredulously and looked again. Yes, he could see the white water breaking over the Walrus Rock, but where was the Goorabinda?

Every vestige of the steamer had disappeared.

Humphry shook the fireman until he awoke him. "Look! look!" he said, pointing out across the moonlit path to where the breakers foamed over the hidden reef.

The fireman looked and gave a gasp. "My oath!" he said, "she's gone orl right! Slipped off backwards and sunk in deep water. There's thirty fathoms just outside the reef. Nice job the underwriters 'll have even to find her now."

CHAPTER XIII

DIVING FOR GOLD

The salving of the specie on board the Goorabinda was a job that presented many difficulties and promised to be long and tedious. The passengers had all been sent on to their destinations, and the major, Finegan and Humphry were all back at their respective occupations for several weeks before the syndicate that undertook the task by arrangement with the underwriters sent their man up to the scene.

Humphry was still lying low and had managed to avoid meeting Major McLean altogether. He remained far away at the boundary-rider's hut, and thither rode Marion Bingham on the grey pony whenever Harold relieved her by staying with Leonie.

Poor Leonie had battled through a terrible attack of brain fever, but her large eyes had still a frightened, uneasy look in them, and her wandering gaze showed plainly enough that she had not completely recovered from the shock.

"But you have no brother, Harold," she repeated again and again when Harold, on his knees beside her couch, explained to her for the hundredth time that it was his brother and not himself that she had seen with Marion in the hut. Still, Harold's explanation was the beginning of her partial recovery, and the doctor expressed the most confident opinion that with care and attention she would eventually be completely restored to health. Leonie never mentioned the subject of Harold's brother to her mother, and Mrs. Linton was so thankful to see her daughter getting better that she ceased to speculate upon the cause of her illness, being content to believe that it was due to a fear that Harold had grown cold to her and had transferred his affections elsewhere—an apprehension completely disproved by the young fellow's devotion.

A certain awkwardness and restraint had crept into the

relations between the major and Mrs. Hesseltine, each of whom was oppressed by the consciousness of a weighty secret belonging to the distant past. The major went less frequently to Mindaroona and spent less of his leisure time on Mrs. Hesseltine's verandah, because the conviction had taken hold of him that he had no right to cultivate the charming widow so attentively when for all he knew he might have a wife still living. Furthermore, he had never quite got over the shock of Muhammad Bahksh's disclosure. It was more than probable, it was almost certain, in view of Shaibalini's revelation to Muhammad and the Pathan's astonishing information conveyed after his struggle with Ah Tong, that the major had a child alive somewhere—possibly a son. If he had a son that son would be now about twenty years of age.

But the major found himself in a quandary. He dared not tell Finegan that he had been married twenty years ago and had reason to believe that he had a child alive, because Finegan was not to be trusted. He was just as likely as not to let out the fact, and if he did so, the major felt that he would not be able to remain at Caringal. What would Mrs. Hesseltine think of him if she found out that he had concealed the fact that he was married, and a father, all those years?

Mrs. Hesseltine, for her part, used to lie awake at night bitterly regretting that she had never told Harold the real story of his birth, but had allowed him and all her neighbours to suppose that he was her own son. She would have to tell him some time. Of that she was certain. And she shrank from the ordeal, postponing it as long as possible, with a dreadful knowledge that the truth must be told some day, and that the longer it was concealed the less excuse there would be for her conduct.

And then she shuddered. People were so unkind, especially one's friends. Uncharitable persons would be sure to put the worst possible construction upon her action. And even at the best, how could she ever look the major in the face again if he knew that Harold was merely a waif whose father was killed by a tribesman's bullet in the No Man's Land between the north-west frontier and the Durand Line before the baby was born, and whose mother had

121

never been seen from the day that she left 'The Cedars' at St. Kilda twenty years previously.

So Mrs. Hesseltine remained obstinately silent, though she saw a reproachful look in Harold's eyes whenever she was with him, which was not often now. She realised with a shudder of apprehension that the boy deliberately avoided her. But, after all, what wrong had she done? It was not a crime for a childless wife to adopt a baby with her husband's knowledge, although not with his consent. Why should she fear the opinions of her neighbours?

And so the widow persisted in her procrastination, but her temper began to suffer, and more than once when Finegan came round to exchange a little agreeable badinage with Jeanie McPherson, he found that young damsel on the verge of tears.

"A canna thenk what's come ower the mestress," sighed Jeanie; "she fair snaps ma heid aff when A speaks tae her an' glowers at me as if A was speakin' Rooshian." So of course Finegan had to console poor Jeanie in the usual way.

Matters on the three stations stood in that way when Captain Baynton, who was Lloyd's agent, arrived in Blackfish Bay on board a small salvage steamer and set about his preparations for salving the specie.

Marion Bingham told Humphry about it when she rode over to see him at the hut, and Humphry at once grew interested.

"I don't know how it is, Marion," he said, "but that Walrus Rock is hardly ever out of my thoughts." And then she saw that the gleam of determination in his eyes was undimmed, and she sighed softly. The search seemed so hopeless and the disappointment of Humphry so certain, that his unswerving belief in his ultimate success was quite pathetic.

"I wish you could give it up, dear," she said, taking his hand in hers, "and let the dead past bury its dead."

"Ah, Marion," he answered quickly, "you must not tempt me to give up the search. If I have little else to offer you, I must at least be able to offer you a name—that is my own. Even the poorest has a right to his own name. But as for me, I am in ignorance of mine. I must know my father's name, Marion, before my life is my own to

122

share with any woman." He buried his face in his hands for a moment, but looked up and smiled when Marion stroked his hair and comforted him.

"I know that I shall some day find out where and how my mother died," he said, "and then everything will be made plain. And I feel that it will be soon. But I sadly need money to carry on the search."

That same afternoon Humphry saddled old Wallaroo and rode down to the little bay where the salvage steamer Grappler was lying at anchor on the lee side of the Walrus Rock. Riding along the beach towards the southern end of the bay, he saw a boat drawn up on the sand and an alert, authoritative man in a thick pilot suit walking briskly towards him, followed by a couple of sailors.

"I say," called the stranger when he had come closer, "I wish you would tell me where the nearest telegraph office is in this God-forsaken place, and how the deuce I can get to it."

Humphry jumped off his horse and gave the stranger the information that he sought. He would have to go to Caringal, eight miles away, and there he would be able to communicate by telephone with Shaleville, where there was a telegraph office that would forward his message.

The stranger thanked him cordially. "My name is Baynton," he said, "and I am in charge of the salvage operations for the recovery of specie lost in the Goorabinda. My diver, I'm sorry to say, has got seriously ill through staying down too long, and none of the deck hands have had any diving experience. Consequently I have to wire to Sydney for another diver."

"I wish you would give me the chance, sir," said Harold under a sudden impulse. "I'm sure I could manage all right in the diving dress." Here was a chance to earn the money that he wanted so badly.

"Nonsense, my lad; quite impossible. I must have an experienced man. Now, the question is how am I to get to this place—Caringal, isn't that the name?—where I can get into communication with the telegraph office. I hardly fancy the notion of an eight miles' tramp."

"You can have my horse, if you like," said Humphry.

Captain Baynton's eyes sparkled. "That's very good of you," he said. "I should like the loan of him immensely. It will mean that I can get back here to-night."

So the captain climbed into the saddle, and Humphry saw at a glance that he was no novice on horseback. Having received explicit directions as to the track to Caringal, he went off in great good-humour, leaving Humphry to await his return and to put in the time by learning as much as possible about the salvage operations from the two deck hands. They shared their bread and beef with him, and having filled their pipes with Humphry's tobacco, became quite communicative.

They both agreed that Captain Baynton was a good man, and that he knew his business. But old Mullens, the skipper of the Grappler, was a fair terror. Baynton had not been able to locate the wreck yet. It must have slipped off the rock and then drifted a little distance before it sank. Hingston, the diver, had stayed down so long that the captain had to administer digitalis and strychnine to bring him round. He wanted to go down again, but the captain wouldn't let him. So there they were. They, the deck hands, were blowed if either of them would go down in the diving-dress. If Humphry could have seen Hingston's face, all blue and deathly when the helmet was taken off, he wouldn't have been so anxious to volunteer for the job.

The hours of waiting passed slowly, but Thompson and Ball, the deck hands, as they lay on the beach smoking, entertained Humphry with strange stories of salvaging at many wrecks along the Australian coast, and of the various fatalities that they had witnessed when the diver's air-pipe got fouled, or sharks attacked him, or an unduly long stay below under the severe pressure caused him to collapse from diver's paralysis.

"It aint the job it's cracked up to be," remarked Thompson, the elder man, with conviction; and Ball, who deferred to him in all things, corroborated with an emphatic "No; that it aint neither."

At last Humphry's ear caught the sound of distant cantering hoofs and recognised the stride of old Wallaroo. It was nearly 9 o'clock at night; and when the captain at last dismounted Humphry saw that the horse was in a terrible lather and the captain in a furious temper. He must have galloped pretty well the whole way back from Caringal.

"Never had such cursed luck in my life," said Captain Baynton to Humphry. "Can't get a diver anywhere. Every available man seems to be on a job, and my people in Sydney wire that they're afraid I won't be able to get one for at least a week. But this spell of calm weather won't hold for a week, and directly the sea gets up I'll have to leave off working. Impossible to take the steamer near the Walrus Rock in bad weather."

"I wish you would give me a trial, Captain Baynton. I'm young and in perfect physical health. I feel sure that I could go down with perfect safety." Humphry made the request with eager sincerity, but Captain Baynton only frowned.

"I could hardly take the responsibility," he answered. "A man needs to be thoroughly fit in heart, lungs, and head if he is to wear the diver's dress without risk to his life." But he looked at Humphry with a shrewd critical and approving glance, all the same.

"I've done plenty of hard work," said Humphrey, "and I'm as hard as nails, captain."

Captain Baynton looked out to seaward, where the Grappler was riding to her anchor quietly. The sea was perfectly calm. It was ideal weather for salvage operations, and there was L20,000 in gold—of which Captain Baynton was to get a generous percentage on all that he recovered—lying somewhere on the bottom of the bay, if he could only find it. He might as well offer this young fellow five per cent. of the specie that he could recover. A skilled man would expect three times as much.

"Turn up here to-morrow morning at 8 o'clock," said Captain Baynton with sudden determination, "and if the conditions are favourable I'll chance it."

So Humphry mounted Wallaroo again, and rode slowly back to Mindaroona through the night, thinking first of Marion's face, then of the resultless search for his long-vanished mother, and lastly of the dangerous enterprise on the morrow to which he had committed himself.

A cold shiver came over him. Was it all to be ended soon—the joy of his new-born love, the unswerving ardour of the search, the fiery ambition to take his rightful place and his rightful name in the world at last? Was it all to finish—next day perhaps—in the short, sharp agony of suffocation down there on the sea-floor, twenty fathoms deep amid the rusting wreckage of the Goorabinda and the spilled gold coins that he had volunteered to seek?

But he was not the man to let such thoughts as these turn him from his purpose. He resolutely banished all gloomy forebodings, and busied himself in laying his plans.

Accordingly, when he reached the boundary-rider's hut he took the saddle and bridle off Wallaroo and turned him out into the horse-paddock. Then he lay down on his bunk for a few hours' sleep, since it was absolutely necessary that he should be fresh in the morning.

Rising at 4 o'clock, he wrote a brief note in pencil for Marion, telling her that he had gone down to the wreck and might not be back for a day or two. He put the note in an envelope, addressed it, and left it on the table, so that Marion should see it when she called at the hut.

After a hurried and frugal meal he set out to walk to the sea, oppressed by the strangest anticipations; and with his brain excited by the thought of the forthcoming ordeal, he almost fancied that he could see his mother's spirit leading him on and pointing the way towards the desolate little bay, on the waters of which the salvage steamer Grappler was peacefully riding.

Just as he got down on the beach he saw a boat putting off from the Grappler. It had evidently been sent to meet him, and before long his two friends of the previous day, Thompson and Ball, rowed in to a sandy patch.

"Jump in, Robertson," called Thompson; "the skipper is just crazy to get to work. He swears that there's a southerly on the way, and it'll probably be here before night, and then we may have to knock off for a week or two."

Humphry jumped into the boat, and when he reached the Grappler saw Captain Baynton walking up and down the deck impatiently and frequently levelling his telescope nervously seaward.

"Hurry up, Robertson!" he sang out; "this flat calm won't last for ever. We must locate the wreck, at any rate, to-day and buoy it. I've been fiddling about here for several days already without getting any further forward, and it's an expensive amusement, as you may guess."

Humphry climbed the rope ladder and stepped down on to the deck of the Grappler, which was crowded with a litter of salvage gear that was quickly being put together under Captain Baynton's orders.

"I sent Hingston home last night, after you had gone," said Baynton. "He went away in a cocky's cart that I borrowed. Not a bit of use keeping him any longer. It would have been murder to send him down in the diving-dress again. His heart had given out."

Then Captain Baynton showed Humphry the gear and carefully explained every part to him. There was the big three-cylinder air-pump enclosed in its teak chest and fitted with two flywheels and handles, to be worked by two men all the time that the diver was under water. There were the lengths of new air-pipe; the helmet, consisting of two principal parts, the headpiece and the breastplate, fitting closely together; and the diving-dress of solid sheet india-rubber covered with double twill and fitted with vulcanised india-rubber cuffs and collar. Then there were the heavy lead-soled boots.

"If you have quite made up your mind to take on the job I'm prepared to employ you," said the captain in his businesslike tones, "and as this calm weather isn't likely to last after to-day, I'd like to begin at once. What do you say to five per cent. of all that you bring up?"

Humphry's eyes glistened as he assented.

So they set to work to prepare him for his descent. When he had stripped to the skin they dressed him in thick woollen stockings, drawers, and guernsey. Then they put on him the heavy india-rubber diving-dress and over it a canvas overall with big pockets for holding the treasure-trove.

Captain Baynton explained to him the arrangement of the valves in the helmet and how to regulate his air-supply in such a way that the air in the dress would float him up to the surface if he wished. He also showed him the electric breast-lamp, which worked on a ball and socket joint, enabling the diver to turn the light in any direction he might desire.

"Now you're quite sure you understand everything, Robertson," said the captain. "Of course, there isn't the slightest danger if you do exactly as I have told you, and in particular if you don't stay down longer than twenty minutes."

"All right, captain."

"What I want you to do first is simply to locate the wreck. Hingston has looked for her already on the east and south sides of the reef without success, so I'm going to send you down on the west side. We'll put you down about five hundred yards out from the reef first and gradually work inwards."

"I'll find her, never fear."

"Of course, as soon as you find her you'll signal to us and come up, and when I know exactly how she's lying and the condition that she is in I can make a plan for getting at the specie. It will be a tough job, for it's right down under two decks in a specially constructed chamber, but I have no doubt at all of our success if you can only find the vessel. It's astonishing how hard it is to find them sometimes when they slip off a reef and go down in deep water. Now, are you ready for the helmet?"

"Quite ready, captain."

So they placed the heavy tinned-copper helmet over his head, and even Humphry's resolute heart beat faster as the segmental screw neck-ring went home with a quarter-turn into the neck-ring of the breastplate, making a watertight joint. The union at the end of the air-pipe was screwed into the valve at the back of the helmet, and Humphry heard a faint singing in his ears as the air-pressure inside the helmet made itself felt.

With the strong life-line fastened about his waist, he stood at the top of the ladder while the Grappler steamed out a few hundred yards to the spot selected by Captain Baynton for his first attempt.

Baynton patted him on the shoulder encouragingly, and Humphry slowly descended the iron ladder backwards.

The water came up to his knees, up to his waist, up to his neck. One last glance round at the sunlight and the upper air and the black plates of the Grappler, then the sea closed over his head.

He stepped off the lowest rung of the ladder and swung by the life-line in mid-water. The water was green and clear. He could see the keel of the salvage steamer. Then that, too, vanished, and Humphry went down, down, down, while the blood sang in his ears and his head seemed to be bursting.

Oh, this was too horrible! A sudden panic swept through him. He must get back to the surface again at all costs.

But the finely-tempered soul speedily reasserted itself and panic was banished by a supreme effort of the will. Downward, interminably downward he sank, and as he slightly opened the outlet valve to regulate the air-pressure a strong jet of air-bubbles escaped and floated up to the surface, whitening the green water above his head.

His heart was thumping hard, more from excitement than from the physical stress of the air-pressure, though that began to distress him, too, when he was 40 feet below the surface. At that distance every square inch of the surface of his body was supporting a pressure of 17 Ib.

At 50 feet it was 22 lb.; at 60 feet it was 26 lb.; at 70 feet it was 30 lb.; at 80 feet it was 35 lb.; at 90 feet it was 39 lb. Could he stand any more of it?

And then he felt the sea-floor under his feet, a rocky shelf trending down to a sandy plain.

As his eyes became accustomed to the dim light of the subaqueous region he could make out the outlines of the rocks and the tall moving masses of marine vegetation that sprang from the interstices. Ah! What was that? The sunken steamer at last!

There she lay with her stern on the shelf of rock and her bow on the sandy plain. Most of the keel had been ground away already by the attrition of the rocks. The steamer was resting on her side, and she had partly opened out, so that she lay like a great half-opened book inviting perusal.

Humphry determined to read the book. Turning on his electric breast-lamp, he threw the powerful beam upon the stern of the steamer. The stern-post was broken away, but there was the solid iron four-bladed propeller.

Humphry bent down and felt it over with his hand. It was iron without doubt and solid — all in one piece.

Slowly he made his way along the port side of the wreck, and climbed upon the deck, which was inclined at a steep angle towards the sea-bottom. The deck was all broken away, but picking his course dexterously, Humphry could see into the engine-room. The engines were heaps of rusty scrap iron.

But the engine-room dial still stood in its place confronting the peering investigator. And the indicator pointed to "Full-speed astern," evidently the last order that had been given from the bridge after the vessel struck.

It was eerie and terrifying down there in the depths of the sea, with the captain's last words still sounding as it were in the ears of the prying interloper.

Humphry began to retrace his steps. But before he left the ship he picked up a heavy spanner and a small rusty axe that were lying on the deck near the door of the engine-room and placed them in the great pocket of the canvas overall that he wore outside the diving dress.

Climbing down carefully over the side of the sunken steamer, he retraced his steps along the sandy patch and mounted the ledge of rock. Then he gave two sharp tugs at the signal-line the signal that he wanted to ascend.

By keeping plenty of air in the diving-dress he lightened the pull on the life-line, but took care to ascend slowly, so as not to bring about too sudden a transition of the pressure. In forty seconds from the moment that he started, the great polished helmet emerged above the water, and climbing the iron ladder, Humphry was safe in the hands of the salvage men once more.

As he sat in a chair on the deck they unscrewed the helmet, and once more he breathed the delicious invigorating breeze from the open sea.

Captain Baynton looked at him incredulously. "You don't mean to say that you've found her already!" he ejaculated.

But Humphry just nodded his head. "You've guessed it right this time, captain," he answered, "and when I get out of these things I'll tell you all about it."

CHAPTER XIV

A SUBMARINE MYSTERY

Captain Baynton's face wore a puzzled expression as he sat in the cabin opposite to Humphry with a number of drawings and plans of the Goorabinda on the table in front of him.

"In the first place, Robertson," he said, "I confess that I am surprised at the position of the wreck in the spot where you have marked it on the chart. I expected to find her much closer in to the reef."

"At any rate, I'm perfectly certain that I cannot be mistaken," said Humphry. "She was lying on her port side with her stern high up on a ledge of rock."

The captain looked at him sharply. "Was the rudder turned to port or starboard?" he asked.

"The stern-post was all broken away and the rudder with it," replied Humphry, "but I saw the propeller—a solid iron propeller with four blades, all made in one piece."

"You're quite sure that it was a solid iron four-bladed propeller," said the captain slowly—"quite clear about that?"

"Oh, quite," said Humphry confidently. "I not only saw it, but I felt it all over with my hand."

Captain Baynton smiled grimly. "Very well, my lad, go on. What did you see next?"

So Humphry gave him an exact description of the state of the sunken vessel, and recounted the details of his inspection. "She was half opened out," he said, "and when I climbed on board I had a look into the engine-room."

"And what did you see there?" asked the captain in tones of dry sarcasm.

"I saw the engines all reduced to rusty scrap," replied Humphry, resolutely looking the obviously unbelieving captain straight in the eyes, "and I saw the engine-room dial still standing with the indicator pointing to 'Full-speed astern.'"

Captain Baynton slapped himself on the thigh exultingly. "Oh, you did, did you, my lad?" he positively shouted at him. "Well, all I can say is that your evidence is of no value to me. Just wait a minute and I'll call Captain Mullens."

Captain Mullens, the master of the Grappler, a burly slow-moving seaman, responded to the urgent summons of Captain Baynton and cast a fishy eye of cold suspicion on Humphry. He had distrusted the landsman from the first.

"Look here, Captain Mullens," began Baynton, "you were on the Goorabinda for over a year as second, weren't you?"

The captain nodded.

"What sort of a propeller had she?"

"A bronze-manganese propeller with each plate bolted on separately," said Mullens in his sepulchral bass.

Humphry turned red and then white. Why did these men want to make him out a liar?

Captain Baynton eyed the young fellow sternly and then began again:

"You attended the investigation by the court of marine inquiry into the circumstances attending the loss of the Goorabinda, didn't you, Captain Mullens?"

"I did."

"What was Captain Black's evidence as to the last order that he gave from the bridge to the engine-room?"

"He gave no order after the tail-shaft broke. The engines were stopped and they never moved again. Before the tail-shaft broke the ship was going full-speed ahead. She never went full-speed astern at all on the day of the wreck."

"Then what should you say, Mullens, if this young fellow says that he went into the engine-room of the wreck where she lies in 15 fathoms of water and saw the engine-room dial with the indicator pointing to 'Full-speed astern'?"

"I should say that he was a d—d liar," replied Captain Mullens, regarding Humphry with a hostile stare.

Humphry sprang to his feet furiously. "What object could I have in telling you falsehoods?" he demanded in a white heat of indignation.

"Can't say, I'm sure, my lad," said Baynton dryly. "It's as big a puzzle to me as it is to you. But it's as clear as the nose on my face that you're a lovely romancer, and that you have no more been on board the wreck than I have."

Humphry said not a word for several seconds, and the two captains stared coldly at him.

The canvas overall that Humphrey had worn over the diving-dress was still in the corner of the cabin where he had thrown it. He walked across the cabin, took it up, and felt in the great deep pocket in the front.

"If I have not been on board the wreck, where do you think I got these?" he demanded with blazing eyes as he flung on the table the heavy iron spanner and the small rusty axe that he had brought up with him from the depths.

Captain Mullens surveyed the implements stonily. "Can't say, I'm sure," he remarked "unless ye took 'em down with ye." And with that Parthian shot he left the cabin.

But Baynton was plainly confounded by the production of these concrete proofs of the existence of the wreck in the place where Humphry declared that he had found it. "Look here, young fellow," he said with an altered manner, "I'm afraid I have done you an injustice. You have evidently mistaken a bronze-manganese propeller with the blades bolted on separately for a solid iron one. And you have misread the engine-room dial, which is quite an excusable error. But I am thoroughly convinced of your honesty now, and I know that you have found the wreck in the position that you have described. Consequently, I am going to ask you to go down again this afternoon and see if you can find the specie-room. Here it is, marked on this plan."

He drew a large tracing over to him and pointed out the exact situation of the specie-room, which was built on to the bulkheads next to the purser's cabin on the port side.

Humphry accepted the 'amende' with a good grace, but he

134

could not forgive Captain Mullens, and he stipulated that that outspoken mariner should not be invited to take any part whatever in the forthcoming operations.

* * * * *

It was just about the time when Humphry had consented to go down again in the diving-dress that Marion Bingham rode up to the boundary-rider's hut and found it empty. But as soon as she peeped in she saw Humphry's note on the table. Why had Humphry gone down to the scene of the wreck? To earn money, of course, at the risk of his life, in order to continue his search in Melbourne for the missing woman, since he had failed to find any trace of her at Mindaroona. Marion instantly determined to ride down to Blackfish Bay herself and watch the operations.

As she cantered past the Caringal homestead she met the major, who was jogging along to pay a call on Mrs. Hesseltine. They rode along together side by side, and Marion mentioned that she was going down to Blackfish Bay to watch the salvaging. When the major turned in at the Mindaroona gate, Marion went on alone.

The major had a delightful proposition to make to Mrs. Hesseltine when he met her on the verandah. Would she get out the motor-car and let him drive her to Blackfish Bay? They might call for Leonie Linton at Yarralla and also pick up Harold. The trip would do the girl good, and it would be an enjoyable and interesting experience for all to see how Captain Baynton was getting on in the work of salvaging the specie in the sunken Goorabinda.

Mrs. Hesseltine was delighted with the suggestion. She hardly cared to admit to herself how much she had missed the major of late, and how much she enjoyed being with him. The incubus of the secret of Harold's birth weighed heavily on her, and she felt sure that the boy himself had in some mysterious way got an inkling of the truth. But she eagerly grasped at the major's invitation, first because of the pleasure that it gave her to sit beside him and watch the unspoken admiration in his eyes, and secondly because it diverted her thoughts from the ceaseless contemplation of her own past actions.

135

If only the strange disappearance of the boys' real mother could be cleared up the path to a frank explanation of everything would be open. But there was something painful and sinister in the abruptness with which that poor Mrs. Robertson had vanished immediately after consenting to give up one of her twin sons. And then Mrs. Hesseltine remembered with an additional qualm that her cheque for L500, drawn twenty years before and payable to Mrs. Robertson, had never been presented at her bank for payment. These memories were dreadfully depressing.

"What an awfully jolly idea of yours, major!" said the lady with one of her most bewitching smiles. "Let's start at once."

So the big motor-car was brought out once more, and the major in the driving seat, with Grace Hesseltine beside him, started off for Yarralla to pick up Leonie and also Harold, who they were quite sure would be there.

Leonie, still wan and large-eyed, was pleased with the prospect of the outing but disconsolate because Harold could not be found. He was not at his usual post that morning. So, leaving a message for him to follow on horseback as soon as he arrived, the major and the two ladies went off in the motor-car, heading for Blackfish Bay.

"That chap Baynton is a very good sort," remarked the major to Mrs. Hesseltine as the car bumped along the rough bush track that led into the main road to the bay. "He was up at Caringal a couple of days ago asking for the use of my telephone connecting with the telegraph office at Shaleville, and I found him a capital fellow—a very shrewd business man, I should think, as well as a good sailor. He gave me a cordial invitation to go on board the Grappler any time I liked and watch the salvage operations. So I thought I might as well take him at his word."

Soon after the car reached the beach the Grappler's working-boat put off and picked up the party of visitors. Captain Baynton, looking through his telescope, had recognised the owner of Caringal and remembered the invitation that he had given him.

Marion Bingham, tying her pony to the fence, joined the

major's party, and the working-boat took them out to the salvage steamer.

Thompson and Ball, the two deck hands, who were at the oars, were full of information, or rather, to be quite accurate, Thompson, the elder, had all the information and Ball, his admiring junior, supplied the corroboration.

But Marion Bingham trembled as she listened to them. What dreadful mischance was this that brought the three persons who were unaware of Humphry's existence to the very place where they would inevitably see him and would just as inevitably see that he was Harold's brother?

"This 'ere young chap Robertson has got plenty er pluck," began Thompson, who was rowing the stroke oar and was in easy conversational range of the party in the stern. "'E comes from somewheres about 'ere too. Ain't wot you might call a perfessional diver at all. Only an amachoor. The cap'n picked 'im up quite accidental like. But 'e found the wreck first pop—didn't 'e, Ball?"

"'E did sure," corroborated the bow oar.

"Ole Mullens—that's the skipper of the Grappler, ladies—'as got the fair nark with Robertson. Sez 'e don't believe the young chap has found the wreck at all. Swears it's impossible don't 'e, Ball?"

"'E do," from the bow.

"But Captain Baynton thinks it's orl right, though the wreck aint ezackly where he expected to find her not accordin' to wot the skipper of the Goorabinda said at the inquiry. Anyhow, he expects to get some of the gold up this afternoon, so you may see the most interestin' part of the job, ladies. That's so, aint it, Ball?"

"Right you are," echoed the bow oar, and then, having occasion to look round over his shoulder to see that the boat was keeping her course, he gave vent to an excited exclamation. "There 'e goes!" said Ball. "'E's going down now!"

The boat was still nearly a quarter of a mile distant from the Grappler, but its occupants could plainly make out the diver in his monstrous helmet and heavy india-rubber

137

dress slowly descending the iron ladder over the side of the salvage steamer.

Marion Bingham gave a frightened little gasp as the polished helmet disappeared beneath the surface of the water. The man that she loved had taken his life in his hand and gone down into those gloomy depths.

"'E ought to be up again in twenty minutes or 'arf an hour at the most," said Thompson, "an' with 'is pockets full of suvverins."

CHAPTER XV

THE SEA GIVES UP ITS SECRET

Captain Baynton gave the major and his friends a hearty welcome on board the Grappler, and proceeded to explain to them the art and mystery of salvage work. "My diver just now," he said, "is an inexperienced hand, a scratch man that I picked up casually, but he has the perfect health and the sound physique that are absolutely necessary for a diver, and I am glad to say that he located the wreck during his first descent."

They watched the two men turning the handles of the air-pump and the third man who stood beside them attending to the signal-line. But Marion Bingham, as she followed with her eyes the white line of the air-pipe where it descended through the water until it was lost to sight, sent her thoughts down with it to the diver groping in the dim underworld. And her heart throbbed and her pulses thrilled as she thought of the courage and indomitable will of the man she loved.

* * * * *

That terrible bursting sensation in the head was not quite so bad during the second descent and the singing in the ears was less violent.

As soon as Humphry's feet touched the sea floor he made his way straight to the sunken ship, and fastened the end of the light line that he carried to one of the deck stanchions. This was the plumper-line, the other end of which was made fast on board the Grappler. A square iron box called a traveller ran on the plumper-line and served to carry up any small articles that the diver might find in the wreck and desire to send up to the surface.

Humphry clambered down again from the deck of the sunken ship and walked all round her, looking for the best way of getting at the alley-way on the port side where the plan of the Goorabinda showed that the specie-room was situated.

He had studied the plan carefully in the cabin of the Grappler. He felt certain that he knew it by heart. Yet it did not seem to coincide with the structural arrangements of the sunken steamer. Was it possible that Captain Baynton had been supplied with a wrong plan?

A strange giddiness was coming over the diver. His heart was thumping much harder now than on his first attempt and he was at a loss to account for it. Still, he would stick to his task and not signal to be drawn up until he had found the boxes of gold coins.

As the sunken steamer lay over on her side and the greater part of the keel had been ground away by the perpetual attrition under the influence of the tides and currents, Humphry found that the line of cabin port-holes on the port side was exactly the height of his head as he stood on the sand outside.

Small fish—yellow-tail, bream, and the blackfish after which the bay was named—were swimming in and out of the open port-holes.

The diver approached one of the port-holes. He would look in and see if he could find any clue. It might possibly be the purser's cabin which adjoined the specie-room.

So the great polished copper head with its one huge glaring eye peered through the rusty port-hole—and saw nothing but blackness. Whatever the cabin contained could only be discovered by entering it from the port alley-way of the sunken steamer.

Humphry climbed on board again.

It was necessary to walk with the greatest care, for the deck was broken down in many places and the diver feared that if he fell through the planking the air-pipe might get fouled, with disastrous results.

Strange how rusted and ruined the sunken steamer was already. Humphry made his way cautiously down the broken remnant of the main companion and found himself in the port alley-way.

140

He entered the first cabin and turned on his electric breast-lamp. Nothing there but the iron framework of two empty bunks. Everything else apparently had melted away.

Leaving the first cabin, he entered the next one. It was a good deal larger, and by the beams of the lamp on his breast Humphry could make out the iron frames of four bunks arranged two on each side and one above the other. Everything that was not made of metal had entirely disintegrated. As the beams of the electric lamp penetrated the dim water, scores of small fish scurried away through the open port-hole, terrified by this intruding monster.

Ha! what was that? A dark object of about one foot square lying on the frame of one of the lower bunks. Humphry picked it up. It was black and solid, evidently made of some metal, and a small key was attached to the handle by a metal chain. He would take it away with him, and Captain Baynton could examine it at his leisure on board the Grappler.

There was something else, too, lying on the bunk. Something hard and round and white. Humphry picked it up and examined it by the light of his electric lamp.

A wave of terror surged through the diver's heart.

How came this ghastly relic of the dead on board the Goorabinda, which had been under water scarcely a month? He seized the metal box and made his way panic-stricken out of the cabin.

Scrambling up the broken companion, he found himself once more on the deck of the sunken wreck. He placed the metal box in the traveller of the plumper-line and pulled the signal-line once.

The traveller containing the metal box rose through the water, passed above his head, and vanished towards the surface.

Again that terrifying giddiness came over him, and his heart beat with a rapid rat-tat-tat that made him sick and faint. With difficulty he clambered down from the deck of the sunken vessel and stood on the sandy sea floor, where strange sea growths flourished in rank profusion.

Oh, that awful feeling of oppression, that terrible weight that was crushing him down, down, down! He sank, huddling, on the sandy ocean-bed.

And then came darkness.

* * * * *

"He ought to be coming up now," said Captain Baynton anxiously, as he stood watch in hand beside the air-pump on the deck of the Grappler. "He's been down thirty-five minutes."

Marion Bingham's face went white. "You don't think there's any danger, do you, Captain Baynton?" she asked.

"I hope not, my dear young lady," said the salvage expert, "but one never knows exactly where one is with novices at this game. I told him not to stay down longer than twenty minutes, but he may have found the specie-room, and he is possibly taking a risk in order to get out the gold."

"A plucky chap, eh, captain?" queried Major McLean.

"One of the bravest men I've ever met," said Baynton briefly.

"How deep did he go this morning?" asked the major.

"Just 90 feet," said Baynton. "It's a very fair depth for a novice. At 90 feet there's a pressure of 39 Ibs. to every square inch of the diver's body, but he ought to be able to stand that much without harm. It's when you go over 90 feet that the risk begins, as a rule."

It was at this point of the discussion that Mullens, the skipper of the Grappler, joined the little group near the steamer's rail. "He's more than 90 feet down now," he remarked sourly. Baynton had seriously offended him by accepting the absurd statements of the diver in the forenoon, and he was not sorry of a chance to even with the expert.

"What are you talking about, Mullens?" demanded Baynton. "I tell you the depth he went down this morning was 90 feet."

"Well, all I can say is that the depth he is down now is 101 feet," said Mullens grimly. "You can see it for yourself on the gauge."

Baynton stepped back quickly, and looked at the two gauges on the front of the air-pump.

The indicator of one pointed just past the number '100,' and the indicator of the other pointed to the number '43 1/2.'

142

"Aint you satisfied?" drawled Mullens. "Looks to me that the man's 101 feet down, and that he's bearing a pressure of 43 1/2 lb. to the square inch."

Baynton's face went a shade paler under the tan. "My God!" he muttered, "I forgot that there's eleven feet rise and fall of tide in this bay, and it's high-water now."

He ran to the signal-line and gave it a couple of sharp tugs. There was no response from below.

"Up with him, lads!" he shouted. "Stand back, please, ladies. Now then, steady; not too fast. The slower he comes the better his chance will be."

They hauled away on the life-line, but very slowly and carefully, so as to minimise the effect of the transition from the areas of greater pressure to the areas of less pressure.

Mrs. Hesseltine and Leonie began to cry, but Marion stood white-faced but dry-eyed beside the men who were turning the handles of the air-pump.

As the luckless diver was hauled up, those on board the Grappler saw at once that he was unconscious—if not already dead. His head had fallen forward, and his body lay like a log in the loop of the life-line.

"Bear a hand there, lads!" sang out Captain Baynton; "look lively now, and get him on board quick."

Two sailors grasped the inanimate figure, one on each side, and fairly lifted the dead weight up the iron ladder.

Locking their arms, they supported the unconscious man in an upright position on the deck while Captain Baynton hastily unscrewed the helmet.

Mrs. Hesseltine and Leonie were sobbing. "Oh, I do hope the poor man isn't dead!" the widow kept aimlessly repeating, but Leonie said nothing. She only passed her hand across her forehead wearily.

Marion alone preserved her self-control perfectly. "I should like to help you if I may, Captain Baynton," she said quietly, though her face was white and her eyes seemed to be twice their usual size.

Major McLean stood beside the girl, admiring her pluck and

presence of mind. In his hand he held the metal box that had come up in the traveller on the plumper-line from the wreck. In the excitement of getting the stricken diver on board, nobody had had time to examine the treasure-trove from the sunken ship.

It took a few seconds to unscrew the helmet from the breast-plate, and all the bystanders stood round with their eyes fixed on that inanimate form in its grotesque dress, supported in the arms of the two sailors.

At last Captain Baynton lifted the head-piece off the helmet, and as he did so, disclosing the blue and livid features of the diver, a wild scream came from Mrs. Hesseltine.

"My God!" she cried. "It's Harold!" She covered her face with her hands and turned away, unable to face the piteous sight.

"What devil's trick is this?" exclaimed the major in amazement to Captain Baynton. "How came you to allow Mrs. Hesseltine's son to go down in the diving-dress?"

"Mrs. Hesseltine's son!" repeated the astounded salvage expert. "This isn't Mrs. Hesseltine's son. It's a young fellow named Robertson, who offered his services to me. I'll trouble you to stand aside now, sir, and let me get to work, or you'll be responsible for the man's death. Indeed, he may be dead already."

As he was taking Humphry out of the diving-dress and laying him down on the deck, there came a hail from the water, and looking out over the rail the major saw the 'double' of the diver seated in the stern of the steamer's working-boat, which had been taken back by Thompson and Ball to bring him off.

"Is that you, Harold?" sang out the major, who trembled with a strange vague premonition.

"Of course it is!" cried Harold cheerily. "You don't suppose it is my ghost, do you, major?" He climbed up the iron ladder and stood aghast at the scene on the deck.

Captain Baynton in his shirt-sleeves was down on his hands and knees working at the unconscious form of Humphry. "Diver's paralysis," he said curtly, and went on moving the arms of the recumbent man up and down. "I've given him a dose of digitalis and strychnine. There is hope yet."

144

And then Harold caught sight of Mrs. Hesseltine and Leonie. The widow gave a cry of relief when she saw him, and Leonie fell on his neck in a paroxysm of weeping. "Harold, Harold! what does it all mean?" she asked hysterically.

"That is my brother Humphry," said Harold in a whisper. "Don't you remember, Leonie? You saw him in the boundary-rider's hut with Marion. I told you that it was not I whom you saw. But I did not know that he was down on the Grappler diving for the wreck of the Goorabinda."

A sharp ejaculation from the major drew the eyes of all to him. He was staring petrified at the tarnished metal box sent up by Humphry from the wreck. He had opened it. Harold went over and stood by the major's side and looked into the silver box of Indian workmanship that sent such a flood of recollections surging through the major's heart.

What did they see in the box?

A ring with a little green stone surrounded by brilliants, a heavy gold bangle with an inscription on the inside, and several papers.

The major gazed at these strange sea-treasures with dazed eyes. He unfolded the papers. The first was a marriage certificate— his own marriage certificate, recording his wedding at Bombay with Mildred Harrington, widow, aged 32.

There were two other papers—birth certificates issued by the registrar of births, deaths, and marriages, Grey Street, St. Kilda, Victoria, recording the births of Humphry and Harold McLean, twin sons of Hector and Mildred McLean, formerly of Tilgit, in the North-west Province of British India.

The major was like a man in a dream. He could not grasp what had happened. But he groped blindly for Harold's hand and clasped it. "My son," he said, "my son!"

And then in an instant he was on his knees on the deck, helping in the terribly anxious work of resuscitation. To find a son and to lose one in the same moment would be a stroke beyond human endurance.

Marion was helping too, and little by little the blue colour faded from Humphry's face, and the faint irregular pulsation of the heart grew stronger and steadier. At last he opened his eyes and they rested on Marion.

"Darling," he whispered, "you have called me back from the great deeps."

Not till then did Marion bow her head, and a warm tear fell upon Humphry's hand.

They lifted him up tenderly and laid him in the cabin, while Captain Baynton, still mystified, looked from the major to Harold and then to Humphry in dumb wonder.

He was still wrestling with the puzzle when Captain Mullens came along the deck holding in his hand the small axe that Humphry had brought up from his first descent to the wreck.

"It wasn't the Goorabinda that he found," said Mullens in an awe-stricken voice. "It was the wreck of another steamer—a steamer that must have struck the Walrus Rock one stormy night just twenty years ago and gone down with every soul on board, leaving no single trace of the disaster. Look here."

He displayed the rusty iron axe-head. It was such a tool as ship's carpenters use, and faintly showing through the rust was a name just legible—ss. Seamew.

"D'ye recollect the Seamew, Captain Baynton?" said Mullens.

"I do," answered the salvage expert. "She was a steamer that traded from Sydney up the coast. She left Sydney one night in October, the year of the Teviot gale, and was never seen again. Looks as if she was coming in to the old jetty at this bay, and old Barnes must have piled her up on the Walrus Rock. I remember the night well. The people on board her couldn't have had a chance. Poor old Barnes! It was to have been his last voyage—and so it was. We often wondered how the old Seamew was lost, and to think that this young chap blundered on to her by accident after all these years!"

"Perhaps it wasn't altogether an accident," said Marion Bingham softly.

In the cabin a few minutes later Mrs. Hesseltine made full confession.

146

The major had found her cheque in the dead woman's silver casket, and the truth was at last made plain. Weeping, the widow told the major the story of the birth of Humphry and Harold at 'The Cedars' in St. Kilda, and how she persuaded the dead woman to hand over one of the babies to her to ease the loneliness and misery of her childless life. "Surely it was not wrong of me, was it, Hector?" she murmured amid her tears. "And I have brought up your son as if he was my own. Will you forgive me?"

Of course he would.

Harold, with Leonie beside him, forgave her too, and so did Humphry as he lay on the bunk in the little cabin of the Grappler, holding Marion's hand in his. He had proved at last that the dead woman was journeying to claim her own child again when she met her death.

And as the little steamer rocked gently over the sunken wreck that was the dead woman's grave, all the fears and misunderstandings of the past seemed to fade away. Humphry and Harold had found not only their mother but also their father, and the major was happy in his sons.

It was the end of the long quest.

CHAPTER XVI

THE DIVER'S TREASURE

When Captain Baynton had recovered from the staggering surprise of finding the long-lost Seamew while he was looking for the Goorabinda, he renewed his search for the more recently lost vessel with redoubled energy. The two divers who came from Sydney to Blackfish Bay were thoroughly experienced men, and they could go down with safety to twice the depth that had been reached by Humphry.

It was lucky for the salvage people that the weather held fair for several days, and before the first southerly came along the real Goorabinda was located in a hundred and fifty feet of water on the east side of Walrus Rock and close in.

When the divers broke their way into the specie-room and crawled in through the narrow aperture between the lower-deck, which had collapsed, and the vessel's side, they found that the sea-worms had already riddled the wooden boxes in which the coin was packed, and the sovereigns and half-sovereigns were lying on the bare plates.

The divers brought up specie to the value of nearly L18,000. The rest of the coin had slipped through a hole in the Goorabinda's plates and had dropped to a depth at which it was impossible to recover it. And there it lay like the gold that inspired the poet Hamilton to write that wonderful sonnet of which the last six lines run thus:

"So lie the wasted years, the long-lost hopes, Beneath the now hushed surface of myself. In lonelier depths than where the diver gropes They lie deep, deep. Yet I at times behold In doubtful glimpses, on some reefy shelf, The gleam of irrecoverable gold."

* * * * *

It was through Finegan that Humphry heard that he had no longer anything to fear from the authorities of the bank in Melbourne, for the real thief had been 'fitted.' A special audit of the books revealed the delinquent, and though Humphry's sudden flight had diverted suspicion from the culprit for a time, it could not save him from the consequences of his guilt. The embezzler was sent up for trial and in due course convicted.

Finegan, for his part, had no desire to return to his previous occupation of jackal for Mr. Con Bounce, of Bourke Street, whose dusty waiting-room, crowded with remittance men and bibulous heirs to extensive estates in the old country, saw the redoubtable Tim no more.

"The major an' Mrs. Hesseltine are to be married just before Christmas, Jeanie," remarked Mr. Finegan reflectively, as he sat with his arm round that young person's waist in the kitchen at Mindaroona, "an' I'm thinking that when Caringal and Mindaroona are joined my boss and yours will be looking out for a married couple to live on the property and make themselves generally useful."

"Weel, Tim?"

"The major asked me this morning," continued Finegan, "if I knew where he could get a trustworthy married couple. I told him I did not."

"Oh, what an awfu' lee, Tim!" said Jeanie reproachfully, shaking her finger at her unperturbed admirer. "Gang off tae him at yince an' tell him ye ken a couple that's gaun to be married as sune as himself, and they'll dae the wark for him better than any ither bodies. Don't stop haverin' here, but gang the noo."

And she fairly drove him from the kitchen to apply for the billet as one half, though not the most important one, of the required married couple.

It was marvellous to see how fast the brightness came back to Leonie's eyes, the rosy hue of health to her cheeks, and the springy grace of youth and happiness to her walk as soon as the mystery in the boundary-rider's hut was cleared up.

"I can't think how I was so blind as not to see the difference,

Harold," she whispered confidentially to him not long before Christmas; "why, his hair is ever so much darker than yours—and he's not half so nice-looking, though of course I intend to like him ever so much as a brother."

Humphry and Marion were not a demonstrative pair of lovers. Nobody saw them wandering together in unabashed abandonment to the happiness of being engaged, like Harold and Leonie. But their love, perhaps, was all the deeper and stronger.

"I never guessed, dear," said Humphry, "that when the search was finished I should find a treasure for myself. And look at this little book of Rossetti's poems that I found in my father's writing-room only yesterday. My mother's name is on the title-page, and father says that Rossetti was one of her favourite poets. Isn't it strange that when I took up the book it opened at this page, and the first verse that my eyes fell upon was this?—

"I looked and saw your love In the shadow of your heart, As a diver sees the pearl In the shadow of the sea; And I murmured, not above My breath but all apart: Ah, you can love, sweet girl! And is your love for me?"

"Yes, indeed it is strange, dear," said Marion; "but, after all, it is only the last of a series of what some people might call the accidents that have brought you and me together. For myself, I find it hard to believe that we have found each other simply through a freak of fate. Don't you?"

THE END

www.ingramcontent.com/pod-product-compliance
Lightning Source LLC
Chambersburg PA
CBHW031514040426
42445CB00009B/219